THE SECRET
LANGUAGE
OF DOGS

D0029513

THE SECRET LANGUAGE OF DOGS

STORIES FROM A DOG PSYCHIC

Jocelyn Kessler

HAMPTON ROADS

This edition first published in 2013 by
Hampton Roads Publishing Company, Inc.
Charlottesville, VA 22906
Distributed by Red Wheel/Weiser, LLC
www.redwheelweiser.com

Copyright © 2013 by Jocelyn Kessler
All rights reserved. No part of this publication may be reproduced
or transmitted in any form or by any means, electronic or mechani-
cal, including photocopying, recording, or by any information
storage and retrieval system, without permission in writing from the
publisher. Reviewers may quote brief passages.

ISBN: 978-1-57174-683-2

Library of Congress Cataloging-in-Publication data available upon
request

Cover design by *www.levanfisherdesign.com/*Barbara Fisher
Cover photograph © Kevin Sherman
Text design by Frame25 Productions

Printed in United States of America
MAL

10 9 8 7 6 5 4 3 2 1

The paper used in this publication meets the minimum require-
ments of the American National Standard for Information
Sciences—Permanence of Paper for Printed Library Materials
Z39.48-1992 (R1997).

My beauties of love and light, you will forever guide me with the same unconditional love as you had when we were together in the physical. I am blessed and honored to be so eternally connected to the limitless light that is you! Thank you Lucy and Lilly, I love you always!

I think I could turn and live with animals,
they are so placid and self-contain'd,
I stand and look at them long and long.

They do not sweat and whine about their condition,
They do not lie awake in the dark and weep for their sins,
They do not make me sick discussing their duty to God,
Not one is dissatisfied, not one is demented
with the mania of owning things,
Not one kneels to another, nor to his kind
that lived thousands of years ago,
Not one is respectable or unhappy over the whole earth.

So they show their relations to me and I accept them,
They bring me tokens of myself,
they evince them plainly in their possession.

I wonder where they get those tokens,
Did I pass that way huge times ago and negligently drop them?

(From "Song of Myself" by Walt Whitman, 1819–1892)

Contents

Preface   xiii

Chapter One:
I Wish My Dog Could Speak   1

Chapter Two:
What Does a Session and the Process Involve?   5

Chapter Three:
But It Is an Animal, Not a Human Being   17

Chapter Four:
Animals That Behave Outside Their Nature   27

Chapter Five:
Animals with Medical Conditions   39

Chapter Six:
Balancing Alpha Energy   53

Chapter Seven:
Rescue Animals and What They Inherit   75

Chapter Eight:
Loss of Identity   93

Chapter Nine:
Opening the Heart Center   99

Chapter Ten:
It's a Wrap   129

Chapter Eleven:
Steps to Connect   143

Appendix A:
Human Chakra Diagram   159

Appendix B:
Chakra Energy and Animal Spirit Chart   161

Acknowledgments

Mom, thank you for your amazing support and love! I am blessed to be your daughter.

Dad, sometimes we just have to *believe,* even when we don't want to. Thank you for all your beautiful support!

Much love and thanks to all my wonderful friends and clients for your support and love . . .

Cathy, thank you for all your support and hard work.

Emma . . . my little "Hybrid" dog, you rock! Just love you!

Much gratitude to my publisher and editor for believing in me!

A *huge* thank you goes out to all the beautiful dogs and their human companions who inspired me to write this book . . . simply a gift!

And the journey continues . . .

Preface

My mother was the first woman to have a Lamaze birth in a strict Catholic hospital in Port Washington, New York. Because this was a rare occasion for this hospital, after the thirteenth hour of labor the word spread of the event and an audience began to take viewing positions in a gallery overlooking the delivery room. My birth had thirty plus doctors and nuns waiting in anticipation to see if this was going to be a successful mission! As the story was told to me, not all the nuns were rooting for my mother. "I don't know why she has to make such a statement. Why can't she just use the drugs that all the other mothers are using?" After twenty hours of labor I was born.

The doctor said I had the rosiest cheeks he had ever seen on a baby. I didn't cry straight away and was quiet coming out. I had a demeanor of serious concern. Only after my backside was given a light spank did I cry. And then, while I was crying, I was placed in my mother's arms, and she said my first look into her eyes spoke volumes: "So, did you give the authority for that?"

Throughout my mother's pregnancy, my parents were the proud companions of a couple of Great Pyrenees dogs. Up until the time of my birth, my fully pregnant mother would walk the dogs daily even through the cold and the rain. Her belly was always resting somewhere near the dogs, and she said it almost seemed necessary for her to do that. I think only now does she truly understand the magnitude and importance of that gesture.

Growing up a very isolated little girl and only child, I very much functioned in a world that seemed, even to me, quite different from most children. Although the dogs were in the house frequently, they were indoor-outdoor dogs who spent a good amount of time in their kennels where they had heat lamps when it was cold. There were many days and nights when I would wander off to spend time playing with the dogs in their kennels until I fell asleep by their side. I was quite comfortable in their arena and spent almost all of my solitary time there. As we moved into a bigger home, we added to our dog family, and, five Great Pyrenees later, my parents started to get involved in showing them.

Because both my parents spent most of their time finding their own places in life, I was left on many occasions to fend and discover for myself. I learned to walk by hanging onto our dog Morgan's big hairy mane. As I spoke his name in very broken English, saying "Moogan, Moogan," my little hands would reach up to hold onto him. He would saunter over, lean his head down, and I would grab on tightly. As he slowly raised his head, I leaned in and began to stand. After I got my footing, Morgan innately knew it was time that Jocelyn was ready to walk. He was there to teach me that.

Funny thing, it seemed natural to me as well, as if that was one of his "job requirements" in raising me. Whether my parents were present or not was irrelevant.

As my little legs scrambled and fumbled for balance, Morgan would slowly walk me from one side of the room to the other until eventually my feet would find the stability they needed. I hung onto Morgan for hours, and when I occasionally fell, I never let go of him. When I tumbled down to the floor, Morgan would just stop, lean down, and lick my face, and I would grab his mane again, and so on, and so on. By the end of the day, I just let go and I was walking. With those first strides, Morgan would start out walking right next to me in case I needed assistance. And then, when he knew I was safe, he just laid down and watched like a proud parent.

Although quite young and not equipped to understand my abilities as I understand them today, I was always aware and puzzled by them. I had more conversations with animals than I did with human beings. When I was upset or confused, I could somehow "hear and understand" what the dogs were saying back to me when I spoke to them. It was clear, crystal clear. Of course, I had no idea then about energy and definitely no idea of communication with forces outside the physical realm. What I did know growing up was that my dogs had the ability to know what I needed before I did. And, that they catered to me on a very spiritual almost human-like plane. It was all I knew. I thought that was how life truly worked.

As I was a very creative little girl with a lot of alone time, I slowly discovered that the knowledge, connection, and energy that I had with animals gave me a lift energetically so that I could see and understand things that made life a little less difficult. During all this exploration, I kept coming back to the dogs. I was more comfortable in how their energy flowed and how clean and clear it was. Whenever I heard what they were saying to me, it was never filled with chaotic detail or misleading emotions. It was always in the moment, clear, concise, and never false.

However, seeing events before they happened, feeling everyone's energy around me, and "hearing" their thoughts when I sat and watched them, scared me and made me feel very alone much of the time. As a little girl with no explanation of what was happening, my mind couldn't quantify it. I was different, and that was a fact. Yet in those days, if you were gifted on a metaphysical level, the first thing that was done was to run tests to make sure there was no "mental inconsistency." With me, all was normal and therein lay the confusion. It is only today that I truly understand it.

As I grew older, I started to identify and work with Spirit Guides, and was introduced to Animal Guides, a form of Spirit Guide. A Spirit Guide is a guide in the Metaphysical world that chooses you and works with you on a higher sensory plane. Historically, the use of Animal Guides dates as far back as the practice of Bon in Tibetan culture. These Spirit and Animal Guides allow me today to partner with them in my process of retrieving or removing obstacles in my energy work with animals and humans.

For many years I was asked here and there to listen to people's animals, to distinguish and decipher what was going on. "What do the animals feel? What do they feel about their companions and their environment?" And even whether they liked blue or red dog bowls. I threw in the color of the dog bowls because all too often the first kinds of questions I received included, "Does she like her brown dog bed, or would she rather have a green one?" I would always giggle because when those questions were asked, the dog's energy would always say, "Is this really what we should be going over right now!" That is when I took a different approach to the process and made it a point to give the dog an equal stance with humans, and focus on what their real abilities were.

The problem was that for a long time, even into my adult years, I had a very hard time grasping my true purpose, and I found it difficult to identify who I was supposed to be. How does what I can do with my energy abilities equate to my life's job or mission? I would be lying if I said it was clear as day. It wasn't. The struggle was incredible and the balancing act was often a losing battle. I found it easier to spend my time trying to ignore my purpose. Somewhat embarrassed, even boggled by how society viewed the whole concept, I was scared to take my avid "side job" and accept it as my main focus, my "real" work.

I ended up in Hollywood, California spending my time in acting classes or working as a writer's assistant. Yet, all the while, I knew I was running and in denial. My "real" work was coming from various entertainment industry professionals who heard that I had the ability to work with animals, and therefore I would be asked to spend time with some of theirs.

I began working with the energy between dogs and their companions, and via that energy along with my Spirit and Animal Guides, conveyed to them what everyone's real purpose was together as a family. I identified the very serious and the not-so-serious elements. And each time I walked back to my car from a client visit, I would feel my most confident, comfortable, and secure.

I found I could move effortlessly in this newly created environment of reading the energy between humans and their animals. Being with animals put me in a place where I was always happy and at peace. I discovered my journey had always been laid out for me.

I am a firm believer in letting go of all preconceived notions and simply trusting. Trusting that if we all just relinquish that tight grip we have on what we believe should be, then the ride will always be much more pleasant. I say this from experience as I had been trying for so long to balance two different lives—the real life's work where I felt at peace, and what I thought was the appropriate part of me to show to the public.

The real work was of course all my many years with animals on a metaphysical level; that is, to connect human beings with their animals using various forms of energy and also reconnecting the human being to himself, so that they are able to get back on track and discover their true journey through the process of that reconnection which, in turn, connects them to the Universe. What I wanted to bring to the public was a talented person who, in effect, was hiding her true talents and gifts. Would those gifts be accepted by a wider audience or would I be as isolated with them as I was growing up?

One day I was having a discussion with a friend of mine, who happens to be a producer, about production assistant jobs. She sat and stared at me very softly and said, "Can I speak candidly to you, Jocelyn?" I smiled and nodded "yes." "Why aren't you pursuing your work with energy and the animals? You have been doing that for so long and have quite a unique gift; why aren't you writing or speaking about *that*?"

I looked into myself in deep contemplation. As the messenger she was meant to be for me, she looked directly into my eyes and asked, "Are you afraid or uncomfortable about how people will view you?" It was the age old question that ran through my mind my whole life. In that very moment I knew she was right. This was time for change.

We are in an era that longs and craves for connection—to something, anything. Without real connection we are lost. When we are lost, destruction and chaos accumulate.

Animals are seen as a lower species, or as household pets, or simply creatures we don't believe have a net worth that can be larger than what we humans presently give them. Animals hold a key that is far beyond what most of us can fathom. That knowledge has always been my mission. And only now have I decided to own it.

I am such a supporter of connection and finding one's true identity, yet I had been doing a severe injustice to myself, to the animals, and to the special gift I was given. I didn't want to "own" or really be friends with my true identity because I was afraid. For me, on a metaphysical level, that "fear energy" wouldn't remotely allow me to move forward. It nearly completely shut off every other avenue of my life. That is, unless it was my energy work with clients and their animals. I made it harder on myself because I let that fear stop the natural flow of energy toward my true purpose. I was forced to identify it–and choose it. That choice led me here—to write this book.

For fifteen years I had two beautiful Basset Hounds, Lucy and Lilly. They were my best friends, guides, and essentially part of my soul. When I would study various energy practices with wonderful teachers, I would come home and do my homework on them. Some of my closest friends are a result of Lucy and Lilly, either while they were with me or, in one case, the topic of a conversation.

They radiated a nearly unimaginable light. When days were tough, I would clear my energy long before going home so as not to transfer it to the dogs. Yet, some days that was hard to do. When I finally stepped into the house, the dogs would run to me like they hadn't seen me for weeks.

When I opened to their energy and was in the moment with them, their energy told me, "We clearly know this was not a good day for you, but you are home now, and it is time to be in THIS moment with us. We are happy!" Literally, it was that easy. That is the truth, and it is right in front of you.

That is what I love about animals. They show us that it is okay to go back to our core nature, which is true raw emotion in the moment. They don't whine, "I don't want to be happy right now because ten bad things happened today and maybe ten more will happen tomorrow."

We have lost sight of that core truth. It's okay to be happy, truly happy, from the gut happy, in the blink of an eye, even if times are horrid. I know it sounds almost inconceivable to some, but that is what an animal can do for us every day of their lives and every day of our lives with them.

Lucy and Lilly were my true educators through many years. As my gifts as a sensitive, an energy reader, and a soul healer got stronger, their guidance is what got me through the toughest moments. When I saw them demonstrating a feeling that was unnatural for them, I immediately looked to myself. When I did that, I saw without a doubt that it was something I was producing and had thrown onto them energetically. Once I was able to identify it, I let it go and, in turn, so did they. They always kept me very aware of myself.

I write this to illustrate that even though I possess certain capabilities that allow me to do my work with animals and humans in an in-depth way, every human being can connect and listen to their dog in a capacity that can profoundly change both their life and the life of their dog.

Lucy and Lilly passed three months apart in what I will say was the toughest year of my life. I was devastated. Yet, it is their grace, spirit, and strength that have elevated my gift and purpose to speak on behalf of animals and their energy connection with human beings.

Now, let's begin.

How to Use This Book

This book is about the metaphysical art of connecting human beings to their animals by using various forms of energy and about reconnecting the human being to his or herself. It describes my energy work with dogs and their human companions, and via that energy and my Spirit and Animal Guides, healing and redirection are provided to both the dog and human. It asks two important questions: How can an animal, your dog, guide and assist you without actual verbal communication? And, what do humans need to do to reconnect to their dogs and become open to receiving that communication? The answers emerge through explanation and education, and through stories and examples of actual sessions with clients. One of this book's goals is to bring much needed attention to the value and appreciation of the wisdom of animals, how they live in the moment, and by connecting to them energetically, how they can guide us to a higher level of understanding who and what we are.

In this book, I use a variety of terms and phrases that are part of my everyday language when doing energy work with my clients, but that may not be a part of your vocabulary—yet. Because many of you come from wide and diverse backgrounds related to knowing and understanding what energy is and how it is received and transmitted, and knowing where there is a block in the flow of energy and how that block is removed during the healing process, the explanation of these terms in the Glossary section of Chapter Eleven will help you develop a better and deeper understanding of the energetic process. I have defined the most often used terms that will provide you with the basics.

I am often asked if there are a few simple steps that allow us to connect on our own to our animals, and by that means to ourselves. To that I say: (1) we all have the capability to connect on a much higher plane; (2) it requires effort, time, patience and diligence; and (3) we must continually stay open, aware, and conscious. For the specific techniques and instructions to connect to your animals on your own, I have included a section in Chapter Eleven called "Steps to Connect" as a guide for your reference. All of the steps make up the "basic approach" you will always use to work energetically with your dog. To work on any specific subject mentioned in the chapters and stories, use the basic approach from Steps to Connect but make your focus and intention the subject matter of the chapter or story.

Chapter One

I Wish My Dog Could Speak!

So often I hear people mutter, "If only my dog could talk. Then I would know what it really wants. I would know what to do!" All the while I am thinking—they *are* communicating with you. They are communicating with you more than you communicate with yourself. That is the problem.

As a society, we are genuinely disconnected. We grasp for anything that could bring us light or joy, and the irreplaceable feeling that we are made of love. We live in a place that fears connection yet pines for it at the same time. You've heard the rant—real connection comes only from you. This, mind you, requires a great amount of work. The excuses fly left and right, and everything else in our lives is prioritized ahead of making the effort to do all the work that is necessary. It is too damn hard to take ownership of who we are and how we behave, so we all stay in that safe disconnected space to which we are conditioned.

That is, unless you have a dog, and not just have a dog, but really love your dog. If that is you, then you may be in more luck than you know! Help is not only on the way, it may be sitting at your feet as you read this.

Animals tend to be undervalued, underrated, and underappreciated. It must be emphasized that all animals of any nature have the ability to communicate energetically. They communicate in the moment and unobstructed, whether dog, zebra, wolf, or horse. This should be remembered and identified as we move forward. However, because the domesticated dog interacts with and around humans, and lives so closely with us in our homes, dogs can communicate on a more in-depth level concerning any of our human afflictions. Most humans do not frequently interact with, nor do they normally live daily with or around, wild animals. I have chosen to focus my book on the interaction, communication, and connection to domesticated animals and not wild animals.

A good example of how connected our dogs are to us is the fact that your dog knows when you are getting a common cold even before you start sniffling. If you have great anxiety, not only does your dog feel it but she takes it on immediately. And, most of the time it's because your dog doesn't want you to feel it.

Animals live in the moment. Once they take on human neuroses, whatever they may be, they have no idea what to do with them. It develops a toxicity that is reprehensible for the animal, and they know that it is not their true identity. When human beings function within all our conditioned issues, we have no idea if those issues are right or wrong, true or untrue; they just are. This is an unnatural state. Your dog, if shown the way, would love to move out of that state instantly and bring you with him.

Unfortunately, we are the ones who refuse to move entirely out of the dark and have become accustomed to the disconnection and conditioning. We have forgotten what it feels like to live in the light. What we don't know is that our dog tries twenty-four hours a day, seven days a week, to have an open connection with us. Our dogs are saying, "Hey, I get you and I am here to tell you we can do this together. Don't you want to live in the moment before you get sick, or divorced, or fired from your job?"

What we need to realize and remember is that an open energy flows between you and your dog, and that what we inflict upon ourselves due to the human condition is transferred energetically to our dogs. Now don't get me wrong. There are many individuals who dearly love their dogs and would never think of intentionally sending any energy that would harm them. However, it does occur.

The most common example of this is the rescued dog, whose life was usually very horrid before he ever came to you. As amazingly wonderful as it is to rescue an animal, the flip side tends to be that whatever may be plaguing the animal is something that has plagued the new human companion for years. Although the dog's past issues that were brought to you when you rescued it are none of your doing, the dog has come to you for a very specific universal reason. It is just manifested in a different way that is not so direct or evident, but is deep-seated and buried within us. In contrast, dogs are so uncomfortable with their affliction that you can see it vividly as it is on the surface and crystal clear.

When I am asked to come and read the energy between a client and their dog, I always connect and listen to the animal first before sending the energy through to the human being. That is because animals are so clear with their energy, and they jump at the opportunity for assistance, whereas the human companion scrambles to detract me during the session or cover up what is really going on. I always say it is never just about the animal. It is always, always, always about the human companion and who they are in relation to their dog.

To uncover and discover this relationship requires an open connection between dog and human companion. Once that is achieved, both souls can be retrieved. The animal and the human being then begin to see one another in a whole new light—a true light that illuminates your dog as a guide, a mirror to reflect who you are, an educator, and a creature who knows you better than you know yourself.

In this way, your dog is the perfect being to show you how to really connect to *yourself.* Through such a teacher, one cannot help but become conscious. The beginning of a new happiness is realized. Energy begins to flow, to move forward, and opens us to limitless change.

Chapter Two

What Does a Session
and the Process Involve?

Throughout the book I will be sharing stories of various clients, like Sonny, to illustrate the process involved and the actual experiences had by all, including me. Since I spent the last five years of my life living and working in Hollywood, many of my various clients come from referrals within the entertainment and other high-profile industries. To keep their anonymity, and the anonymity of all my clients, I have changed their names and the names of their animals. An example of a form of disconnection is the story of Sonny.

Sonny

Prior to meeting a new client, I always ask the human companion not to provide me with any information other than the name of the dog, and so, I had a name only—Sonny. For days leading up to my visit, I felt pressure in my heart. The pressure indicated something was trying to open up—burst, if you will. As I brushed the energy aside and cleared myself, I knew I was going into a very interesting and special case.

When I arrived for my visit with Sonny and his human companion Steve, I immediately received informational energy about who this dog was. As I approached the front door, I took a breath and became instantly open and yet protected at the same time. I knew the issue was a Heart Center connection, and that both Sonny and Steve needed to bridge a gap that existed between them.

Sonny, a boxer mix, was rescued about six months prior to Steve contacting me. Steve gave me a smile as I stepped in, and his energy was hesitant with a hearty dose of skepticism. I instantly bent down and acquainted myself with Sonny. I tend to go right to the animal before really acknowledging the human companion. I am there for the dog, horse, cat, or whatever the animal may be, and my real relationship begins with them.

The energy between Sonny and Steve was flat, very much like that of a boss and his assistant. When Steve spoke to Sonny, he was always very matter of fact. Steve wanted me to see he had everything together, and that Sonny should know that as well. The funny thing is, every time Steve gave Sonny a command, Sonny glanced up at me with such an expression that if he could have shrugged his shoulders and shaken his head, he would have. The look was, "See what I am working with here?"

Steve began speaking in his orderly fashion, attempting to control a situation over which he had none. "Where do you want to do this? Pick a room, I mean where do you need to be? How about here? How about over there?"

I always try to calm the human companion with a quiet and easy voice that assures him that everything is okay, and this is not by any means a hard process. So, as always, I suggested a room or area of the house where the animal, as well as the human companion, would feel comfortable—a place where we could sit on the floor and just spend a little time together.

We decided to sit on the floor right outside the kitchen on a rug that Sonny loves. I always begin with the statement that sometimes it can take a moment before the dog will start really opening up. I surrounded myself with my own guided assistance. Once that was accomplished, I asked through the use of energy for Sonny's guides to come in. Some days it can be an instant beginning, and on others we may have to sit for a bit. I try to relay to every client that, although we live in a world of instant gratification and zero patience, patience is a full-fledged requirement throughout the process. We can't watch the clock ticking here.

Sonny came over and sat on my lap. Now, mind you, this is a good-sized dog. His warmth is overwhelming, and when you touch him, it is nothing but sheer joy. Literally. Every animal is different, and not all are overwhelmed with sheer joy at the moment of first real contact. This one was.

As Sonny and I merged, I could see and feel the energy travel between us. I closed my eyes and saw Sonny's heart and Steve's heart. Then I saw something that looked like a cinder block wall encompassing Steve's entire Heart Center. And then there was stagnant static energy—fixed, still, unchanging, and motionless—as if a six-foot fence of static was revolving around Steve, pulsing around him.

Although Sonny was a rescue, he generally didn't have any neuroses of real concern (no sickness, issues with his food, or real material or physical needs that were not being given to him). He had a good mother who did the best she could. He didn't get much food as a puppy, which, by the way, seems to be a standing issue with most rescues.

Sonny let me know he came to Steve for one reason only: so Steve could learn, in the second half of Steve's life, to love something again. Steve had been severely hurt and traumatized from loss in the past. Sonny's reasons for coming to Steve were to let Steve know he did not need to feel alone, and that his heart is actually alive, well, viable, and capable of feeling unconditionally again. Sonny was there to revive a heart that was really no longer living.

Sonny sent the energy that he is nothing but patience, *real* patience. He was sent to Steve to endure the many days, months, or years it might take for Steve to really let his heart feel again. Sonny was so thankful that Steve, as hesitant as he was, felt the energy from Sonny to come find me. It was certainly very lovely to witness, and a pleasure for me to share in the experience.

Every animal wants you to love them, and they want to love you. That is never in question. But remember, there are often so many things they need to work on. Quite often, their issues are the same hidden issues the human being needs to discover and release from the dark confinements of the mind. The energy and the message are different for every case. However, in every process a Heart Center connection is made that allows the light to shine for both. In this case, Sonny was sent to Steve to restart his life, not only for Steve to learn how to love again, but how to love Sonny as himself and then eventually to love another human being. That human being could never arrive unless Sonny succeeded in his task. Quite a beautiful thing. Sonny was Steve's guide to give life to a deadened heart.

"Steve, did you have some significant loss or trauma, maybe in the last couple of years?" I asked. "I am getting that it was a lot of trauma or loss. One hit after another that left you desolate and numb." As I looked up at Steve, he had a sad but concerned smile. "You are smiling; am I off base?"

"No," he replied. "I am shaking my head because you are right." He was shocked that I could immediately go there, but again, it isn't as if that's where I choose to go. It is where Sonny and the energy led me. It is where they needed to attack. In fact, it was really all they needed to attack.

I then gently broke all the news to Steve that Sonny shared with me—about Sonny living in a backyard where he was semi-confined, that he lived most of his earlier life outdoors, and that food was not exactly plentiful. I asked Steve if he knew whether Sonny lived on a farm of some sort. Sometimes the energy, when it only wants me to focus on one thing, will give scattered information without much detail, so I am forced to ask the human companion questions to clarify. At that point, the energy can get a bit more focused and I can decipher the information being sent to me.

Simultaneously, there is also energy coming from the human companion, saying, "This is what I want to know: I want to know where he lived and what he did." Yet, in this case, Sonny knew the only real information he wanted to impart to Steve through me was that we must mend Steve's heart and quickly.

"Steve," I asked, "do you find that sometimes you feel as if you are living in a box of static?" He nodded "yes."

I continued, " . . . as if nothing new is happening; business is at a standstill; no communications coming in or really going out; deals postponed or disregarded entirely; and no drive or motivation? In fact, perhaps you are altogether rethinking your line of work. And when you reach out, you can't seem to touch anything really tangible in your life. You are at a complete and utter standstill. Does that sound right to you?" As a couple tears inched down Steve's face, he again nodded "yes." Sonny ran over to comfort him.

"You are afraid to really connect to Sonny," I told him, "because he could die or be taken away from you. That loss, considering what you just experienced not too long ago, is something you cannot possibly imagine enduring again. Yet, when you adopted Sonny it was an instant thing. You knew right away, gut intuition, no debating. Sonny was just sitting quietly waiting for you and only you. Do you know that?"

Steve let me know that was exactly what happened. He went to a couple of rescue centers with a friend, and when he saw Sonny, he knew; he didn't need to think. He was in the immediate moment. Very much like an animal. He knew at his core, without any thought, that this was it. Sonny was able to penetrate the static force of energy Steve carried that no one else knew how to see through.

Sonny and Steve knew this was the moment, the time, the beginning of change that would alter the whole next half of Steve's life. Sonny was ready for the job and was just waiting for Steve to be ready. Sonny let me know that he was already prepared to do whatever was needed for Steve and for himself. It is so very rare to find this in human nature. The majority of us do not have the capacity to think this way. That is what an animal, in this case a dog, can do for someone who is willing to work on that level. They can quite literally change the whole course of your life.

At this point, it was time for us to get right into removing the block and the static, and then retrieve the soul from both Sonny and Steve. I do this differently for every case, but what stays consistent is that the energy goes in, as asked, and retrieves and mends what is needed so the souls can become bright, alive, and live vibrantly again in both the human being and the animal.

I laid Sonny down and rolled him over on his side. I put my hand on his heart and let it rest there for a moment. Sonny's eyes shut, and a beautiful calm took over. His heart was beating full and strong. Sonny, the energy, Steve, and all the guides that were with us were ready for Steve to connect and reopen his heart. I kept hearing that Sonny's heart was to become one with Steve's, which meant the strength and openness of Sonny's heart would breathe life into Steve's.

I called Steve over and had him lay his hand on Sonny's heart. I then put my hand on top of his. Steve definitely had an air of skepticism and a look on his face that said, "this is beyond ridiculous." I never let that bother me. I always keep moving with what is necessary for the process. As Steve's hand rested on Sonny's heart, I sent my energy through both of them, internally asking for assistance from my guides to open their hearts and bring the connection.

After a moment, I removed my hand, and it was just Steve and Sonny. Steve's eyes started tearing up. He smiled and said, "I don't think I have ever felt his heartbeat. Wow. What an amazing thing. This is so beautiful. I can hear it, feel it. It is so tranquil and lovely. I think he likes it too!"

I sat for a while as Steve felt so content where he was. He couldn't pull his hand from Sonny's heart. Once he did, I said, "Your heart is now open and connected to Sonny's. Sonny will watch over it, and while I am not here, he will let it grow, keep it full and open, and aid in its healing. You are lucky because this dog only came to you with one real intention—to let you have a heart again. Perhaps a new person will come into your life, or new projects will start coming in, or you will have great new successes again. The static field of energy you traveled with is lifted, and a new flowing energy can now propel both of you forward. Sonny is unconditional and has the patience to wait beyond your wildest dreams for you to really love him and allow a connection. So it is not just having a dog. It is opening up to the possibilities of a real life again and to see what having a full heart can bring."

As Steve took his hand off Sonny's heart, the two of them were content and happy. I could see Steve's heart without the obstruction and free from static for the first time since I had been there. It was beating as one with Sonny's.

A man who had everything he could ever want had been walking around missing what felt like everything. And in essence it was. It was his heart. Sonny and I helped him find that. Now he is at the beginning process of learning how to take care of his newfound light and learning not to guard his heart so much as trust it. Let it feel without fear. A very difficult process for a human being, but one that is effortless for Sonny.

As soon as I walk through the door, I instantly start connecting to the energy of the animal, the house, and then the human being. The dog's energy provides me with what the dog wants from the human companion, why they came into each other's lives, and the psychological state of the dog and human companion while they're together. Simultaneously, my abilities as a sensitive pick up what has taken place in the house, relaying both good and bad events, who has come and gone over time in the home, the nature of the relationship that exists between the human companion and the animal, the childhood of the human being, and what she dealt with growing up. And of course, I can't help but notice the nervousness the human companion always demonstrates when I arrive.

It is very interesting walking into a new home under these conditions because, as the human companion is making small talk and the dog is running under my feet, I am already flooded with information I have just begun to decipher and put together. At first it was sometimes confusing and overwhelming for me. When that occurred, I tried to slow down the energy flow until I could really sit and connect. Now, I let it flow without a fight because eventually all of it will fall into place.

I am a big proponent of not lingering. Whenever I work with an animal and the human companion, or just the human being, my practice is to not cling to anything. We remain so long in disrupted energy and then want to talk about all the reasons we need to stay in it. "What about this? What about that?" It is at that point I say,

"Let's acknowledge it, move this energy out, and get rid of it. If you want to let it go, fill the space with light and feel refreshed, loved and alive, then let's go for it." Justifying and talking about the reasons over and over only fuel the disruption and are frankly a waste of everyone's time. Especially when working with a dog who says to me, "How long does he really want to hold onto this because I certainly don't? Can you just help us move this away so we can get back into a natural light and into the moment?"

When the souls of both the animal and human are ready to be retrieved and the light energy is linked, the bond is so transforming you will do everything you can to remain there within its illumination. That is the ultimate goal. Now we are *human,* and unfortunately certain circumstances exist that can alter us and bring us out of that moment. It's natural and doesn't warrant belittling yourself. We do that enough!

So how does this actually work? How do we remove the obstacle energy and retrieve the genuine soul? Well, it is much easier for me to accomplish this with an Animal Guide because your animal is your guide and your biggest supporter of the journey—the one that will keep you in check once I am gone. We can do the work with just the human alone, but when I leave, it becomes the individual's sole responsibility to keep themselves in check. This takes a huge amount of courage, strength, and consistency, and you will need to continually remind yourself of one thing—as with all events in life, including the process of soul retrieval, mistakes in judgment may be made, or you may let yourself down. It's part of being human. It's part of life.

The retrieval process requires you to stay conscious of you, your dog, and the energy, no matter how silly you may think this is (and believe me, I have had people not hold back and let me know they think just that). It is the same group of individuals who are too scared to take the leap. If they have a dog, the animal and human being have virtually no connection. In addition, the human usually has problems connecting to anything, including loved ones, friends, office mates, parents, and so forth. The list goes on. Most importantly, they have no connection to *themselves*.

Chapter Three

But It Is an Animal,
Not a Human Being

Many times I hear people say "It is an animal, not a human being," and I have to bite my tongue so as not to attack the entitled individual who sprayed that comment in my face.

Join me on the life-changing journey of Gidget and Norman's discovery of living in the moment together for the first time.

Gidget and Norman

The distinction between an animal and a human being is what makes us different by nature. This natural distinction does not need to be viewed solely as a form of separation because our dogs can have a strong influence on us, and we on them. The story of a dog named Gidget is a good illustration of how the power of an energetic connection can strongly bind together an animal and a human to create a partnership based on a state of energetic equality.

Whenever I approach a new client, I am probably more nervous than they are. My protocol is to get very little or no information about the animal or their human companion before I arrive at the session. The reason for this is that often for days leading up to the visit I feel a strong pull energetically from the animal. When this occurs, I have to constantly remind myself to step out of that energy and keep a clean energetic slate. This allows me to not form any preconceived energetic assumptions prior to my arrival. In this particular case, I was not only excited to meet Gidget and her human companion Norman, but I purposefully quieted my mind at least two days before our appointment.

This part of my process proved to be even more necessary because Gidget is epileptic and has severe motor issues resulting from a degenerative brain disease that affects her movement, control of her body, and her ability to control her own mind. The challenge for Gidget and Norman is very great because this is a disease that will never go away and over time can slowly shut down Gidget's whole body unless Norman and Gidget can learn to calm and control the energy of their minds. It has never been more important than now for these two to understand how to do that!

Nothing impresses me more than observing and working with a dog that has trauma or disease and, in particular, trauma that targets the brain. It is so amazingly beautiful to watch the effortless grace and light that these dogs exude as they struggle to maintain their natural state and stay in the moment where they are healthy, instinctual, and free to move. This process should be no different for human beings. Yet for us, life takes hold and we can lose our way. We become disconnected, and our mind and thoughts become clouded, distracted, and unclear. As a result, I am determined that my visit with Gidget and Norman is about one thing and one thing only—how to take the power of the mind and the energy that fuels it, and control it! And just as importantly, to control it through Gidget's and Norman's Heart Centers in order to connect their Heart and Mind.

In Gidget's case, it *is* a matter of life and death to redirect the mind's energy, reconnect to the source, and understand how to use the mind to heal and create calm. I know everyone is now saying, "I don't know what the hell that means!" Well, as we get into their story, I will do my best to explain that process as my visit with Gidget and Norman was one of the most touching and beautiful experiences I have had in a long time.

The beauty and grace that dogs and human beings share never cease to amaze me. One heals the other, even in the toughest of times. The energetic connection between dogs and their human companions can transform lives, and that process surpasses all logic as we know it! Let me introduce you to the beautiful angel that is Gidget.

Gidget and Norman have many similarities. Although Gidget has epilepsy and Norman does not, Norman also has the inability to control his mind and has what I refer to as a mind that is "settled" and "stale." What I mean is that Norman's mind is so overloaded with disruptive thought that it has been nearly impossible for him to dig out of the dark cloud of unhealthy energy within his mind. He is flooded with the effects of the "human condition" and with neuroses that he has taken on from many other people in his life. This unhealthy mind energy is a core issue shared by Gidget and Norman although for different reasons and from different sources.

When I use the term "core issue," I am referring to a very specific deep emotional issue that has existed within the animal or human for a very long period of time, and due to its magnitude, has stopped the animal or human from moving forward beyond it. In this case, Norman and Gidget's unhealthy mind energy is a shared core issue that demonstrates the disconnection between their Heart and Mind Centers. Said another way, the source of Norman and Gidget's Heart/Mind disconnection is their lack of confidence and trust both within themselves and in others.

Every dog comes to her human companion for a reason, and vice versa. It is up to each one of us to truly understand why these unions occur. For Norman and Gidget, theirs is an illustration of the magic of life that has brought them together—a connection that has been orchestrated like a fine symphony. Norman would like to stay in the moment and get his mind to connect to a higher energetic level. Norman *needs* to learn that from Gidget. Although her disease doesn't allow Gidget to continually stay in the moment, it does come naturally to her as it does to all animals and she can teach that to Norman. In addition, Gidget is clear of any negative energies or disruptive patterns except for the unfortunate disease she possesses. Gidget needs to quiet her mind and redirect its energy. Gidget *needs* to learn that from Norman once he is healthy minded and reconnected. Understanding how to energetically reconnect to themselves and then to each other, and at the same time gain the trust and confidence needed to get control over the power of the mind, are not easy tasks for Norman and Gidget. This one Universal lesson that brought them together requires them to see each other equally energetically in order to succeed. This is true for not only Gidget and Norman, but for all dogs and their human companions.

The challenge for me in my work with Norman was to get him to connect to himself, to Gidget, and then to the Universe in order to become healthy. In this way going forward, Norman could in turn assist Gidget with her disease. My mission was to teach Norman how to get quiet within himself and with Gidget when they journey out together on a walk. I noticed Gidget was able to become very clear and quiet in mind when she was energetically led to do so. As I walked Gidget with that clear quiet intention, she no longer fell to the left or to the right. Whenever she started to sway as we walked, I stopped her. Then I took a deep breath, became completely neutral and clear, and sent that energy through to Gidget. Gidget responded beautifully and began to walk normally. She absolutely *loved* it as it allowed her to just be a *dog* in the moment and not a dog that was sick and struggling. For Gidget, if she won the struggle with her mind, then she had succeeded!

I taught Norman how to delegate the energy of his mind so that he became clear and quiet while out walking Gidget, and to make that his intention for himself and for her. I also taught him how to energetically release and connect when he felt he was straying from the moment. "Delegating the energy of the mind" is no different than delegating your energy from day to day. You must decide how quickly you move thoughts in and out of your mind, how you want to process those thoughts and why, and then ask to be released or made clear so you can stay connected to yourself.

The biggest eye opener was when Norman turned to me and said, "I am starting to feel disconnected and my mind feels scattered." Seconds later, Gidget fell down and started to sway uncontrollably while they were walking. As we stopped, Norman adjusted and quieted his mind. We began again, and Gidget regained her balance—not wavering once. In this way, both Gidget and Norman could enjoy their time free and clear of an erratic mind.

The beautiful thing about all this is that in our short time together, Norman learned what it was to become energetically *aware,* and both he and Gidget benefited tremendously from that energetic awareness. We must take a look at what challenges us energetically so that we do not give our minds the upper hand as the "boss," so to speak. You, your energetic source, and your connection to yourself become the *real* boss!

As I packed my bag to leave, I saw Norman and Gidget looking at each other very differently. There was a sense of renewal for both of them. Then Norman turned to me and said, "I think I understand who Gidget is. Although I know she is my dog and we are two different species, I feel as if we are so very much one and the same. I guess it's as if I am open and connected to her soul's energy, like we are energetically woven together and connected. Does that make any sense?"

I smiled and let Norman know that was the ultimate goal. Becoming energetically aware is *always* the first step to opening up to anything and everything you want to work on within yourself and then with your dog. "I am so proud of you and Gidget taking this step together and understanding the magnitude of the Universal partnership you share." I bent down and kissed Gidget's soft head and then gave Norman a hug. "This stuff isn't easy," I said. "Knowing how to move and refocus the energy of the mind is not for the faint of heart. But knowing you have a solid partner, a friend, and a family member fighting for the same cause, the battle starts to not feel like a battle after a while, and life begins anew!"

I walked to my car, got in, and sat there for a while before starting the engine. I needed to bask a moment in all that is Gidget. Her bravery and beauty needed a private moment of recognition from me before I pulled out onto the busy streets of Los Angeles. When I was ready to put the car in drive and proceed, I was lit up by the fact that, yes, she is an animal, and not a human being.

All too often we take a higher stance and place ourselves in the position that, as human beings, we know more, see more, and can do more than animals. Historically, the animal kingdom has been looked down upon as an inferior group we can control and dominate. The funny thing is, I have found that the answers are within animals. If we could remove our dominance, we would find that the quiet animal kingdom is full of guidance and assistance. They want to help. They want to become one with us and not be considered less than.

In the domesticated genre, the dog is widely held as "man's best friend" and is exactly that. Like every other animal that lives in the moment, dogs can detect the truest form of meaning. They possess an understanding that is unclouded, without excess baggage or thought, and they are our closest resource to clarity.

How then can an animal, your dog, guide and assist you without actual verbal communication? What do we humans need to do to become open to receiving that communication?

It is actually quite simple. First, we must listen and clear our minds, our thoughts, and the relationship we have with our ego. Most often when I suggest this to clients, the response is the same. "Well, it isn't that easy to do because it is not only one thing I have to deal with; there are many problems, and they are so difficult to get rid of." My answer here will be the same as when I answer a client: it *is* that easy.

The elimination of an unwanted condition is effortless if you fully don't want it anymore.

I have found this to be true whether I work with animals and humans, or human beings alone. The core problem that is identified connects to all the other issues we manage to drum up. This initial "virus," if you will, has a long string of other smaller organisms that grow out of it. Then our minds feed on this feast, and we become conditioned. We are comfortable like this. There is a food source. We could choose to get out of this conditioned space, but damn it, we are going to take it with us on our travels so we can let our minds refuel from it as long as possible. Then, when we are done, we store it so we can build on it again, and let other organisms form around it in the many little closets we have in our minds—all of which are overwrought and way too full to begin with. In contrast, animals do not keep "closet space." They have no hidden agenda taking up storage. They don't even know how to "store." Their issues are prevalent and in your face, and as a human companion you distinctly recognize them on a daily basis.

If we were to let that food source go, where on earth would we *feed*? What else could we complain about or fret over? What would replace it, if anything? Could we still function, or would we be empty? Well, to that I say, look at your animal!

For example, when an animal is admonished for causing trouble, no more than ten minutes later—when the opportunity to go for a walk or chase a cat or run after a squirrel appears—BAM, just like that, the emotion disappears and a new moment begins. Yet, under similar circumstances, as human beings we allow ourselves to become clouded and preoccupied. A friend might say, "Do you want to go to a movie?" We say, "No, I don't feel like it. I am down tonight." Or, "I need to be alone." You get the gist. The dog will always choose light and happiness over anything else.

When clueing into your animal, you might think, "He looks sad. He is upset. It's probably because I went jogging by myself last week and didn't take him along." That is not true at all! You are guilty about that; it upsets you, and that emotion and energy have now worked their way to your dog. The longer we hold onto it, the more we transfer it to the animal. The dog is doing what a dog does—he looks at you with those eyes that are saying, "I want to go jogging with you because I love that, and I am smart; so, if I sit here looking like life will end if you don't take me jogging, then you will!" That is a natural state and perfectly acceptable, as are many other wonderfully natural actions dogs take. This is because dogs are domesticated animals that exhibit natural domesticated actions.

There is a problem if your dog runs and hides in the corner and sits there with a somber spirit because the dog thinks you will not take her out jogging. This kind of behavior occurs when the energy given by the human companion and the anxiety picked up by the dog have brought the dog into an unnatural state (more fully discussed in the next chapter). In this instance, the human energy was unnatural because there were so many more issues than, "I am not taking you jogging." It is, "I am not taking you running because I am worried about various issues in my life, I need alone time, and I don't need to be preoccupied by you. All I need to do is run on my own."

This type of problem usually occurs when the human energy is dark. Construed in reality, the only reason the person doesn't want to bring the dog is because they know deep down inside that the one real light source in their life, who has rescued them too many times to count, will, without even trying, force the person to identify the absurdity of their actions. Of course, if there is anything a human being dislikes, it is being around anything that forces ownership of their actions. As a result, the dog stays home.

In this example, I am sure the dog "communicated" over and over to the human companion, "Listen to me. You don't need to live in that moment. Let's get rid of it. Let it go. Let's just run together and live in the moment of real light."

Very few individuals can live in the core of the moment as an animal can. We brush aside moments and ignore the change of energy, an energy that could not only change that moment in time, but the course of a whole day, a week, a month, or a year. We will let a human being change life events for us, but to even think, as much as we love our animals, that they could possibly have the capacity to do the same, seems absurd.

Chapter Four

Animals That Behave Outside Their Nature

When a dog behaves unnaturally in response to any neurotic, chaotic, or disruptive energy taken on from humans, he tends to look confused because he has nowhere to put the energy that is reverberating within him. He doesn't really know why he is acting out, nor does his behavior make the least bit of sense to him. This is not to say each animal doesn't have unique personality traits or actions that appear to be very human-like. Again, as a human companion, you recognize your dog's uniqueness daily. The important thing, and part of what my job entails, is to discern whether the energy around your dog's behavior gives him joy and comfort, or confusion.

For example, a companion might say, "I don't know why my dog scratches her face until it bleeds. We know she doesn't have any allergies, and we have taken her to the vet all too often to inquire about this." It bothers the dog companion when the animal's display is puzzling.

That's when the animal is showing you that some sort of toxic energy has taken over, and the energy has been in the works, churning and churning over a certain amount of time. The dog is confused and in misery over it. So the initial reaction by the companion is to see if someone can fix it.

An illustration of an animal who was uncomfortable in mind and whose behavior was puzzling and troublesome for his human companion is the story of Stanley and Nancy.

Stanley

When I first approached Stanley's house, the energy felt very "contained." By contained I mean it was neither good nor bad. It had no flow to it. It just hovered, waiting to decide to move. A little like Dr. Jekyll and Mr. Hyde. It's always worrisome because good or bad is a crap shoot. The energy could switch drastically at any moment when it no longer needs to be contained.

I knocked on the door a couple of times and waited. All the blinds were down so I couldn't see through the windows. I knocked two more times, and then waited a few minutes more. As I started to get my phone out to call, the door opened.

"Hi. So sorry. Stanley and I were resting. I said to Stanley, if you hear Jocelyn, wake me up. He must have slept through your knocking."

As soon as Nancy finished her sentence, I saw Stanley walk in very slyly and lay on her feet. Then, he looked up at me and through his energy said, with a little sparkle in his eye, "I knew you were there at the door the whole time. I just want you to know that."

Stanley absorbed three very different energetic identities that complicated his state of mind. Because Stanley was a rescue, the first was a mixture of the human energy he had been around before he was adopted. The second developed after spending three months with Nancy during which time Nancy actively energetically supported the neuroses that Stanley brought with him, some of which were very significant. Finally, because Stanley is exceptionally bright, the third identity was of Stanley's own creation as he took on every new neurosis in his environment, shot them up with steroids, and took off running like the Tasmanian Devil.

The states of mind that inhabited Stanley were very confusing for him. His condition was so amplified that he couldn't even understand whether he really loved the moments of joy more than the moments of discipline. He had not been able to find his natural state and identify his true self, which caused him tremendous anxiety. He was so lost in one moment that he couldn't possibly grasp the next. That is a very unhealthy and unnatural state for a dog, and Stanley was its victim.

Within only two minutes, the quiet little Stanley lying in front of Nancy's feet jumped up and ran into the kitchen, grabbed a piece of bacon off the kitchen table, added one of Nancy's shoes to his mouth, then split out his doggie door. All that confined energy was released, and this was exactly what I needed to see.

Nancy yelled for Stanley. He ran back in with her shoe in his mouth along with a piece of rubber he had been chewing up from the garden hose. Nancy turned to me and said, "This is what I need help with."

I suggested that if we just sat there quietly together for a bit, I was sure Stanley would drop everything and sit down as well. As we both sat on the floor in front of Stanley, he dropped what was in his mouth. I asked him to please sit with me. Stanley walked slowly over to me and lay on my legs. His whole body was shaking from adrenalin until he finally calmed down and looked at me.

I told Nancy I was going to quietly do a little energy work with Stanley before starting the reading. It is not what I usually do, but this was a very different situation. Stanley was crying out for help. He wanted balance, and he really wanted me to help heal him. He loved Nancy, but she never gave him boundaries so that he could obtain a middle ground. It was always all or nothing—on both sides—and he was frankly exhausted.

His anxiety was also causing digestive issues, excessive chewing and biting, as well as the weekly expense of hundreds of dollars for shrubs that needed to be replaced because Stanley had ripped them out of the garden.

Stanley lay on his back while I worked on his nervous system. I worked at a fairly strong pace to rebalance his mind. I did this by focusing my energy through his Crown Chakra (the energy center located at the top of the head that oversees the brain), specifically in the direction of Stanley's nervous system. I put myself in a meditative state. I used my left hand (my feminine side because Stanley was too fired up with masculine energy), and placed it on the top of his head. I placed my left ring finger on his Third Eye Chakra (the energy center which is in the middle of the forehead), and then placed my other fingers and the thumb of my left hand around his head with my focus on his left brain hemisphere. I set my intention to remove the static neurotic behavior flowing through his nervous system. It was energetically flowing just as caffeine runs amok in our nervous system when we have had too much coffee.

At that particular moment in the session, I did not ask for much help from Stanley's guides, which appeared to me during meditation in vision (interestingly enough, they came to me mostly as monkeys). Instead, I used one of my Animal Guides that has been with me for quite some time. Without going into any specific detail, it is basically in the form of an elephant. I asked for the elephant's assistance because it is slow and steady. Elephants move with great intention, and they don't move in haste. They are gentle and this was a wonderful source of energy to use as I calmed down Stanley's nervous state. I sent a visualization through white light of the slow, calm, unobstructed energy of the elephant into Stanley's left brain hemisphere. That slow-changed energy moved from Stanley's brain through his nervous system to slow him down and make him less aggressive.

At times throughout this process, Stanley would start flinching and struggling, letting out little whines. He did this when I had a good lock on removing the energy source causing the neuroses that he was so accustomed to. Stanley was so confused and lost that he was having a hard time letting go of the neuroses that kept him so nervous and unbalanced. The energy was screaming at me to leave it in place, and Stanley himself was saying, "I don't know how to function without this. I need it just a little longer." It is very rare for a dog not to want an immediate release. Most animals identify what I am doing, breathe a sigh of relief when I arrive, and actually look forward to my visit. However, Stanley quite liked the anxiety he received from his foster family and the fact that it was held over by Nancy.

I worked on Stanley for a good half hour. Nancy sat quietly next to us on the floor. When I was done, Stanley went into full submissive mode—on his back with his legs effortlessly dropped to his sides. He lay there looking at me as I said to him, "Welcome back!" It took him about five minutes to roll to his side, get a drink of water, and come to the middle of our little circle. There was simultaneously energy of relief and fascination. And then he took a nap.

I said to Nancy, "You are afraid of Stanley and have accepted his spurts of severe irrationality that come in many forms, whether it's chasing shadows or problems with certain lights being on. You don't stop the energy, you step into it. Because you don't know how to deal with it, it gets dismissed. Then you leave Stanley in it." Nancy shrugged her shoulders and admitted she did that. "Many times I thought that maybe I chose the wrong dog, that I couldn't handle him. He is young, yet so riddled with these terrible bouts of behavior. He has no socialization skills and is terrible with other dogs." I could hear the concern in Nancy's voice. She wanted to help, she wanted to know what to do, but most of the time she couldn't be bothered. In those moments of dismissal, Stanley's behavior was actually being encouraged by Nancy, and his neuroses were given even more energy.

Stanley was primarily kept in the house all day with only a backyard to roam through. He was not given any walks, and had no real connection to anyone, let alone a connection to his true self. Stanley's energy told me that disconnection was also one of Nancy's main issues in life. She makes a point to never truly connect with anyone, not even herself. In her state of disconnection, she can function without really feeling or dealing with anything to its fullest potential whether business or personal.

I further discovered that Nancy was hurt emotionally when she was younger and grew up in a family that didn't avidly work through anything. There is nothing unusual about that; it tends to be common with many families. However, Nancy fell into a trap and couldn't connect on any level that required work because then she would be forced into ownership, which is difficult for many people. So instead of dealing with those issues, Nancy decided to get a dog. And so, in walked Stanley.

I asked Nancy, "Did you really feel a connection to Stanley when you rescued him or was it something else that drew you to him?" Nancy sat there for a few minutes, thinking quietly. "I just thought he was so cute and he looked like he would be fun." I then told her there were a couple of reasons Stanley came to her. First, he was drawn to her through her subconscious, which told her, "You don't really have to connect to him because he is a dog you can just 'own.' He will do his thing, and you will have something to come home to, but you never really need to do anything for him." Nancy lived alone but didn't spend much time at home, and when she was home, it was as if she still wasn't there. On the other hand, Stanley chose Nancy because he knew he could continue his chaotic behavior while at the same time he would be taken care of and would no longer have to live in a foster home.

Nancy was like a toy Stanley could love who would reinforce anything and everything Stanley wanted to do.

Yet, when Stanley spoke with me after I worked with him, he was clear in voice when he said he wanted Nancy to truly connect to him, invest in him, and that perhaps, in turn, Nancy would do the same for herself.

I encouraged Nancy to walk Stanley often and to enforce boundaries in the home for both Stanley and herself. Stanley wants Nancy to start having more fun in life and to really live! He is the perfect companion to guide her in that direction. However, in order for Stanley to be healthy while doing so, Nancy needs to be diligent in her efforts to not "feed" Stanley's erratic behavior. He can lead a healthier life with a clear mind and clear connection to his soul if Nancy's energy obliges and restrains from contributing to that behavior. Nancy will have to become fully aware and conscious for that to occur. In turn, Nancy will have a calmer dog who will now breathe a sigh of relief that he has returned to a clearer state of mind—one in which he can cleanly move from one moment to the next and not exist in an energy over which he has no control. This will force Nancy to be cognizant of herself, her actions, and her energy, which in turn will connect her to Stanley.

This series of new events has the power to balance everyone's mind. Nancy can have the true companion she really sought, and Stanley can still have all his wonderful energy to run, play, and do so many cute and wonderful things. As Nancy enjoys Stanley, she learns to enjoy herself. Then a union is truly formed.

Nancy agreed she knew it was time for a significant change. I could see the struggle in her eyes. She was entering into a new time of her life, and having me there is always the first step toward change. I commended her for that.

I always feel so proud whenever I get called to a new client because they never really know the wonderful step they have just taken. That choice alone moves the course of energy into a whole new direction. It happens instantly and quickly. Therefore, I always make a point to praise anyone I work with because I know how exposing and difficult this process can be. The hardest step has already been taken. Now the work begins, but in a very different way. Stanley takes ownership, then Nancy takes ownership, and a new beginning has begun. Neither is alone anymore.

It is important in life, whether you are dealing with a situation such as this or any other situation you do not understand and which could go either way, to approach it with neutrality. It is no different with energy—that is, always approach any energy that has the ability to instantly be either good or bad with a neutral state of mind.

If we are neutral, and we do not have an investment in either side, the good or the bad, then we are more open to seeing how to move through the energy being contained. This applies to decisions in the work and home environment, or the energy of an animal that is stuck hovering and contained between two energetic forces. It is in those moments that I always choose neutrality.

How does one become neutral? Simply put, one does not invest in the outcome. Just maintain the clear intention to accept either calm or chaos, and then take action from there.

For example, energy is contained and hovering when we first come upon a wounded animal. Let's use a wounded bird. We don't know if, as we approach the bird, whether it will be aggressive and bite us, or whether it will lay quietly and somehow know we are there to help it. It could go either way. If we remain neutral, we can decide what action is necessary in the moment. And remember, the bird itself (or the dog, or any animal) is always in the moment.

Another approach to an energetically contained situation is that we do not need to inject ourselves into the situation at all. We can choose to just observe and stand outside it. This is a method I like to use myself, and often teach it to be used in everyday life. It requires grace, quiet, and the ability to release any entitlement to the situation.

That is neutrality.

Identify the Problem

By all means I encourage a trip to your veterinarian for any sickness or for any symptom that needs to be checked. I am not suggesting that all unnatural behavior is only energy-related and shouldn't be under the care of a qualified professional veterinarian. What I am suggesting is that no matter what may ail the animal, even one that is being treated medically, the condition is often easier for the animal to bear if we also remove the disruptive energy that could have contributed to it.

I am sure there are many animal companions reading this who are thinking back to certain moments they had with their dogs, cats, or other pets—when they were first told by the animal that the animal was being pushed out of their natural state. The animal looked to the human companions to listen in order to connect. It's important to note that we cannot over analyze or get technical here about how we understand if our animal has moved out of its natural state. That's just not going to work.

When one asks me how I know when an animal, in this case a dog, moves out of its natural state, I will always ask this: "How aware are you of yourself when you move out of your natural state?" It is often so easy for the human being to say, "I am just not feeling myself the last few days." You notice that your energy level is low, perhaps you are acting in ways you don't normally act, and that is confusing you. That is easy to identify, right? You want to give the time to be aware of yourself.

In this case, being aware is your key to being aware of when your dog moves out of its natural state. It takes just a few extra moments to really notice that your dog has veered into a space that seems perplexing or out of the ordinary, no matter what the change is. Dogs do not sway in and out of a natural state effortlessly, as humans do. Therefore, it is easier to see if your dog has in any way started to act erratically if you are connected to your animal. It is no different than when you notice that your own energy is different.

Here's an example. Your temperament has changed due to everyday stress, or a large workload, or anything that might throw you off kilter, and you never do anything about it. You just give the excuse, "It's a tough week, and I'm a little out of sorts." I will guarantee you that your animal will feel that change in energy. You will notice that he may be a little more highly activated when you come home (or, in the same condition as you are). If your animal is a dog, he may take on one or two new little tendencies that you have not noticed before (such as behaving more aggressively, being more destructive, getting into the trash, or chewing household items excessively). All of this is general mischievous destructive behavior that is annoying to a human and which you cannot help but notice. Now, if this is not "usual behavior" for the animal, the first finger of blame points to the dog. "What is wrong with my dog?" you say. In response to that, your erratic behavior, your change of schedule, and how you are handling the stresses in your life are affecting your dog's natural state—which is unobstructed and certainly not erratic.

I will say this: now is not the time to beat yourself up over this. Do not let your mind run through all the times you may have neglected your animal or may have been living in a selfish, neglectful time of your life. "Why didn't I see that or feel that?"

This is another wonderful lesson that animals teach us: to *not* beat yourself up over anything or go back to the past. The past is the past, nothing more. Animals do remember things, smells, and feelings, but that doesn't hinder their progress to move forward and own the moment. We human beings do that.

Chapter Five

Animals with Medical Conditions

Many times I am called by a human companion to work with an ill dog. After I tune into the animal's energy, I next work up and through the human being's energy. When I do this, the dog lets me know automatically and right up front that the human companion has certain issues going on in her life that are very serious and that made it hard for both the human companion and the dog. Although the dog's illness was a marked destiny in time, the treatment and the communication of it to the human can sometimes become blocked. By the time the human companion, the dog, and the vet become involved, the energy has erupted into a cloud of chaos, and the real or right moment for resolution is nowhere in sight—thus, the tale of Ruby and Buddy.

Ruby and Buddy

This was an interesting case on many levels. There were two dogs. One had several health issues that were being treated, and the other was a vivacious young male who did not know how to bide his time while his sister received all the attention. I was walking into a situation that involved not just a single human companion, but a newly married couple. I was informed I would be meeting with only the wife, Carol, indicating to me that the husband wasn't fully present on a day-to-day basis. In place of the husband would be Carol's mother who, I was told, was already highly skeptical and abundantly suspicious. The mother apparently agreed to go along with the reading considering that her daughter, at this point in her life, was grasping at straws.

Carol's life was overwrought with responsibility. In addition to a very demanding job and a new husband, she had two large dogs that required a lot of attention. The female, Ruby, had to be brought to the vet on a weekly basis for treatment. I was made aware of this from Ruby's energy, brought to me the day before walking into their home, along with the fact that Ruby was feeling the brunt of Carol's mother's energy, which was bursting at every seam. All of this disruptive energy was not aiding in Ruby's recovery, nor was it protecting Ruby from any other outside force she might encounter.

I knocked on the door. I could hear the ruckus of two large dogs barking and running through the house. I started to smile because it sounded as if Carol was keeping elephants in there! The energy came streaming through the door—erratic, nervous, not moving forward or flowing, but circling at high octane speed, bumping into the walls and everything inside them. You could see sparks flying everywhere when the door opened. It was quite amazing to see.

Carol answered the door, looking frazzled and wide-eyed. She was nervous and tired. When I shook her hand, I could tell that the real Carol had taken a trip into this vortex of disobedient energy that was running amuck through her life, her home, and her animals. Her eyes were saying, "Please help me, I am trapped and I can't get out."

As most human companions do, Carol started making apologies for her dogs' behavior. "Please excuse this, please excuse that." I gave Carol a hug and reassured her everything would be fine. I advised her to just take a deep breath, use the time while I was there to not worry about anything, step into my energy, and see what it can feel like to see straight for a moment.

We found a common room liked by the family, Ruby, and her brother, Buddy, and we sat down. Carol was opposite me on a long couch with Ruby sitting next to her. Buddy ran out the dog door to try to release the pent up energy he had from spinning within the vortex that existed within the house.

As Carol's mother walked in for an introduction, she was exactly as I had expected. Her energy was hard, brazen, and resistant—my way or the highway mentality. But, there's nothing I like more than a challenge.

"Hi, I'm Jocelyn, so glad to be here," I smiled. Then I started to move her energy out without her being remotely conscious it was even being done.

I asked for Ruby to come sit by me so I could start tuning in to her. I like the animal to not be obstructed by any human energy while I have my hands on the animal. It interferes with the process and makes it much more difficult for me. Yet, there sat Carol's mother on the other side of Ruby, as if she were holding court. Her hand was petting Ruby's back while I was holding Ruby's head and moving my hand along Ruby's chest. Before I knew it, I could hear Ruby, my Guides, Ruby's guides, and the energy in general saying very loudly that the mother had to move away. She threw great amounts of negativity into the energy stream, and in that moment was doing a great injustice to the animal she seemed to love.

"Okay, so I need no other hands on the dog while I am working on her. Perhaps if you are comfortable to do so, you could go over and sit by your daughter, at least until I am done connecting with Ruby. I love that you are supporting Ruby, I do. But I feel your resistance toward me and the process. That's fine. I completely understand where you are coming from. However, I am here and try-ing. So if we can be as positive as possible through my visit, I think we could all work together. Does that sound like it could work for you?"

Carol's mother smiled and her guard fell. She moved away from Ruby, and out of nowhere, became part of the process. We formed a circle of love and happiness for Ruby, Carol, and Buddy who was still outside running back and forth, barking and pacing. We were ready to make a change.

Right off the bat, Ruby was more worried about her human companion and caretaker than herself, which is always how it works. The energy is always, "Please fix my human companion. Identify the issues I am telling you about and then you will be able to help me. Because my human companion's issues are making them unhealthy and I am already unhealthy. So, if we are all unhealthy, then where does that leave anyone?"

I was rubbing Ruby's stomach and looked up at Carol. "Does Ruby have digestive issues or bowel issues?" Carol shook her head "no." "Really, because I keep getting terrible digestive bowel issues that are causing head pain and discomfort. Are you sure she doesn't have anything like that?" Carol again shook her head "no" and said, "Not that I know of."

I focused on the energy more. Something wasn't right. I knew in my gut that I was hearing other than what Carol was acknowledging. I continued to rub Ruby's stomach, then around to the lower spleen, and I got it! "It's you, Carol, that has the problem. Do you have Irritable Bowel Syndrome?"

Carol's eyes welled up with tears and she said, "Yes. My God, how did you know that? Did she tell you that?"

I kept going. "You get terrible migraines?" Carol shook her head an adamant "yes." "When you go to load Ruby into the SUV once or twice weekly for her vet visits, as big as she is, you have to struggle so much, and you are in such pain that the headaches become migraines. Your lower back is sore and pulsing, and your IBS elevates to near unbearable levels of discomfort. Plus, I understand you don't bend at the knees or ask for help . . . ever. Does that sound right?" Carol's shoulders dropped, and her eyes were sullen and heavy. She was exposed. It was time to get better. It was time for ownership.

I noticed Ruby always looked to Carol for reassurance, always. That was a sign of a dog that lacked confidence, which was a sign of Carol's lack of confidence in herself. Ruby was not necessarily looking to Carol for her own reassurance but to see if Carol was okay. Carol needed that from Ruby because no one else in Carol's life was doing that for her—most importantly, Carol wasn't doing it for herself.

For Ruby, what were already hard visits to the vet were made even harder by the serious difficulties Carol had when putting the dogs into the car. The fact that Carol is so overwhelmingly stressed and in pain causes anxiety in Ruby and sends Ruby into a very uncomfortable tail spin—of nerves, fear, and anxiousness. None of this can possibly be beneficial for Ruby when she is going in for treatments for a serious ailment. Ruby wants Carol to be well, to be able to take the precautions to be in the moment, and to feel good so that Ruby can feel good.

I told Carol, "Ruby doesn't love the weekly visits to the vet, but she doesn't get upset about them. She gets upset about you and your anxiety. Ruby takes on your energy, which holds her in an energy field that is frightening." Ruby had a tough enough time finding her confidence and had received so much of Carol's neuroses on top of her own medical issues that she had almost been swept out of being a "dog." Ruby lost her identity, and ironically, so did Carol. They needed to reestablish their individual identities together.

To avoid the energetic injection of Carol's medical condition onto Ruby, Carol needed to separate her energy from what is her condition and what is Ruby's condition. On many occasions, Carol made her medical condition Ruby's medical condition; and in response, Ruby made her medical condition part of Carol's medical condition. It is always up to the human being to take ownership of what belongs to her and what belongs to her dog. This is especially true for an animal that has severe medical problems and is highly vulnerable and open to all diseased energy. In these types of animals, in this case, Ruby, the dog's immune system as well as energetic system cannot fight against her own issues let alone the issues thrust upon her by her human companion.

Much too often we human beings believe everybody and everything should feel everything we feel, and share it with us. Breed it more—make us feel as if we can swim in it. I am saying it is time to take responsibility for our own victimization and not think we need to share it with others, especially not a weakened animal. Dogs are not victims, and giving them energy rife with victimization when they are already vulnerable to wanting to please us is the most detrimental thing we can do to the animal. If we do this, it will put them in our unhealthy state added to the unhealthy state they are already in.

We therefore must separate our energies and not project our illnesses upon our dogs. It is from ego that we do this because we don't want to be the only one that feels bad, and our dog is the easiest scapegoat and a convenient target for the negative destructive energy we feel. Energetically and physically, a dog can never (and doesn't have the capacity without human conditioning and intervention) go into a victim state; only humans have this capacity.

As connected as Ruby and Carol were, I needed to get them back in a loving, happy, natural state where they could be in their own space with a clear, lovely, flowing energy that allowed them both to breathe and tackle life in a calmer and more natural way. In this natural state, the energy actually has the capacity to heal and bring new opportunities for both of them. I removed the blocked energy, carefully brought light back to Ruby and Carol, and gracefully instilled it throughout the house.

It is important to remember that life will always have issues and things that need to be dealt with. I am not saying that all is bliss once the energy is changed and your original light is retrieved, but I will guarantee this: If you can recover that lost "soul" and see some ray of light where before there was nothing but overwhelming stagnant energy and nothing worked, then as obstacles come up, they will be dealt with from a very different source, one that originates in clean energy, in the moment, and you will find yourself responding only by intuition and from your Heart Center.

In the case of Carol and Ruby, their whole lives were affected: Carol became happier and more productive at work. Ruby can really be with her brother Buddy as a true dog and have involvement that makes her feel free. Carol is open to learning how to manage her health, she feels good about it, and her health has actually gotten better. Whenever Carol needs to deal with a real problem in any part of her life, she will now have the ability to deal with it in the moment and let the newly found clean energy pass on the difficulty. She will no longer be subject to an energy that corrupts her, slows her down, or takes her away from her true self. Even though I didn't know Carol prior to that first visit, I knew she had abandoned that light a long time ago. Ruby knew they could find it again together for both their sakes.

Carol and I spoke about different herbal approaches that were noninvasive and would not hinder the medication Carol was already taking for her IBS. As always, whether for a human being or an animal, I recommend asking your physician or veterinarian if my suggestions are approved. I usually do not suggest anything other than certain foods or my wonder drug—ginger root. This is because I don't feel it is my place. I don't take that authority, it is not what I do, and I do not want that role.

I avidly suggest various scented oils to be placed on the temples and wrists, oils that can, just by their aroma, bring a human being or an animal back into the moment. Making one conscious by scent stimulation is remarkable. It is a very interesting concept and tends to work. I suggested a specific oil to Carol that, through her energy, she would respond to when needed. The scent would bring Carol back before she let the energy become chaotic or lost track of the soul we had retrieved.

Next was good ol' Buddy. Buddy is a "dopey" dog with a heart of gold. One of those dogs with a demeanor that everyone would describe, in human terms, in the same way: "Just a really good guy!" That's Buddy. Buddy has no problem with his sister's issues or his human companion's issues, but he doesn't understand why he can't get a little more attention. If that isn't feasible, then why can't he get back this one toy he loved so much?

You see Buddy is a big dog, a mutt of sorts, who has a lot of anxious energy because he wasn't being put to use. He didn't know why he couldn't go to the vet all the time to be a support system for Ruby as well as Carol. As I told this to Carol she started to laugh. She said that he often wants to come. However, she thought it would just add to her pressure so she leaves him at home. The energy that was circling from Buddy to Carol was that Buddy wants a *job!*

Carol treats him as "happy-go-lucky Buddy," but he is actually a great resource as a companion and assistant to Carol when she undertakes the hard trips to the vet or when she needs a laugh after a long day. She wasn't using

Buddy for his real essential purpose. Whether human or animal, who doesn't want someone like Buddy—an easy friend with a happy outlook, one who wants to help and who has very few issues of his own—in their life? Buddy doesn't take on Carol's or the family's issues; he travels completely in the moment, and his soul is not remotely in need of retrieval. Personally, I am still looking for someone like that!

Ruby felt that her brother didn't play a large enough role in her life. She wanted to be more like him, a carefree goofy dog whose light is so bright it lights up the yard at night, a being full of confidence and security that is through and through a dog. Ruby was truly amazed by Buddy.

After I did Ruby's reading, and we were all talking, I watched Ruby observe her brother playing outside with a twig. Ruby longed to do that. She was so burdened with medical issues and Carol's issues that had become her own, that she almost questioned whether she had the right to long for playful things. Ruby constantly looked to Carol, over and over, before doing anything, whereas Buddy never checked in because he didn't need to.

I thought it was a good idea to next bring both dogs outside to put into effect the work we had done inside with Ruby, Carol, and her mother. As we went into the backyard, Ruby ran along Carol's side with the occasional burst toward Buddy to get in a little bit of play. Always, though, Ruby returned to check in with Carol. You could see in Ruby's eyes that with this new feeling running through her all she really wanted to do was play. I then asked Carol to let me change Carol's energy. As she stood in front of me, I moved the excess "baggage" aside and

advised her to be conscious of living in that moment—
the moment where she felt whole and complete. I asked
her to not usher Ruby back to her side for reassurance,
but rather let her energy reassure Ruby that it was time
for Ruby to step into the world she longed to be in—that
of being a dog. In that same moment, Ruby ran toward
Buddy and started wrestling and playing with him with
gusto, something she had not felt in some time.

Carol later admitted that because of Ruby's medical
conditions, she was controlling Ruby to resist playing so
that Ruby would not overdo it. Believe me, I understand
this concern. I have been there myself. However, controlling Ruby's amount of recreational play in a small backyard compared to completely abolishing it were two very
different things.

What Carol was now aware of was that her own anxiety and confusion had been taken on by Ruby and had a
force over the dog that wasn't part of the healing process.
Rather, it was an imposed energy that didn't allow Ruby's
sickness to dissolve. Unconsciously, if Carol kept Ruby
in the energy of ill health, then she could keep herself in
that exact same energy. Under that circumstance, neither
of them would experience any movement. They would
remain within the energy of the vicious circle that was
created—continually unhealthy and suffering together.

Ruby so desperately wanted out of that circle. Carol
gave her a present by bringing me in and opening herself
up to the process from which everyone, including me,
benefited. Ruby couldn't have been more proud or grateful to Carol than at that moment.

Ruby bounded around the yard smiling and tus-
sling with her brother for forty-five minutes, never once

checking in with Carol. Ruby knew when she had played enough. She could monitor her own energy, and knew when she needed to lie down for a bit. When Ruby lay down, so did Buddy—right next to her. He honored her and understood her because she was clear and present. He knew exactly what she needed. They lay together butting heads, cuddling, and playing with a ball they passed back and forth.

Carol and her mother were amazed by the beautiful happiness that was radiating from Ruby as she played with Buddy. Carol said she had never seen them so happy when they were together, and Carol also felt an abrupt change of energy within herself. It was remarkable. Carol was able to just sit and talk about life and not be preoccupied with Ruby. The light around Carol reappeared, and as her eyes got brighter, so did her soul. Carol's once skeptical mother was now feeling the same joy—she couldn't help but be affected by the process.

As I was sitting on a step, Buddy suddenly ran up to me and placed all 100 pounds of himself on my legs. He wanted to have a quick little chat. He thought since we were at it, he could get in a couple of words—like a child who sits on Santa's lap and asks for something you hadn't heard about before. That was exactly the experience. He again let me know that sometimes he doesn't get enough to do (which we had already established), and that he liked a particular toy that makes a bunch of noise when he squeezes it. It occupies him for hours. It is his most favorite item ever, and Carol took it away from him months ago. He wanted it back.

I looked up at Carol and said, "Did Buddy have a round toy? It seems to be a bright green rubber-like toy that has what appears to be little things poking out all around it, like little rubber spurs of some sort." Carol's eyes start to widen. "Anyway, I think it was one of those very obnoxious noisy toys that Buddy would put in his mouth, squeeze, and run around with all day long. I guess you got sick of the noise, but he really loved it. It helped calm his mind when he was left alone, and it was a sound he loved to hear when he ran around the yard. Anyway, he said you abruptly took it, and hid it. Is that true? He would really like it back!"

Carol stood up and had me walk inside with the dogs. She opened a closet, moved several boxes out of the way, reached up to the top shelf, and pulled out a bright green round rubber toy with little spurs poking out from all over it. Carol let me know that months ago she got fed up with the noise, took the ball away, and hid it. She was in awe that Buddy let me know that. Yet, it didn't surprise her because she knew how much he loved it.

When she took it down, I asked her to call Buddy over. I told her to ask Buddy to sit, let him know it wasn't a punishment, and with clear energy tell Buddy that as Buddy works with her and Ruby, so too will Carol work with him. Buddy saw the toy. His eyes were like a child's. As though, after the message was relayed to Santa, the present instantly appeared. Total and utter magnificence!

As Carol handed the toy to Buddy, I sensed from him that he felt reconnected to her. That moment was so instant and joyful for Buddy, and it radiated to Carol. The noise and his use of the toy were no longer to compensate for any anxiety. The toy was an old friend, something he loved, with nothing else attached.

Then Ruby ran over and Buddy showed and shared his toy with her. His eyes lit up. At the same time , Carol turned to me and said, "Thank you." And, in unison through energy, so did Ruby and Buddy. It was Christmas in July. Everyone got exactly what they wanted, including me. I felt blessed to have been a part of this journey. I walked to my car, elated that this family could experience the joy they had all along.

Chapter Six

Balancing Alpha Energy

I often walk into situations where an alpha dog is ruling the other dogs and its human caretakers—essentially everyone in the household. On those occasions, I have just crossed into the "Alpha Bureaucracy."

Taking that phrase apart according to Webster's: *Alpha* is the first letter in the Greek alphabet and the chief star in a constellation. Bureaucracy is excessive official routine run by administrators who apply the rules of their department without exercising much judgment. When it comes to the human-dog world, you now have your worst nightmare . . . a dominant, aggressive, and controlling canine inmate running the asylum!

Billy and Lila

As I drove down the windy canyon road to my appointment with Billy and Lila, I kept feeling a tightness in my heart and a desperate need to open all four windows in the car and just take in the warm summer air. And with each breath, emotion would bubble up. Emotion that was very new to me yet somehow familiar at the same time. I knew it didn't belong to me. It belonged to the household I was quickly approaching. When I am en route to a new client, I try to stay calm, even, and open, not jumping to analyze anything that starts to come up. Clear, clear, clear—that is my personal motto before stepping into a new home environment. Yet no matter how much I moved aside any pre-conceived senses, the one thing I did know was that I was entering an environment in need of freedom and a chance for both human and dog to live without every breath being controlled and monitored. That was something I could not ignore.

I parked the car and walked slowly to the front door. I knocked a couple of times and waited patiently for Jasmine, the human companion of Billy and Lila, to answer the door. Suddenly the door flew open and standing in front of me was Jasmine, dressed beautifully in a bright yellow, long silk caftan adorned with gold and turquoise necklaces. I definitely felt underdressed for this session!

After a hug and a sincere hello, we sauntered into the house. I looked down at my dirty jeans and torn t-shirt (with the coffee stain on the front that I didn't notice until that moment) and started to feel not very put together, to say the least. That feeling was very out of sorts for me, yet understandable because within this home there was clearly a compulsory sense of order—a code, so to speak, to which everyone living under the roof complied, most particularly any female within the home, be they human or dog. I realized that the energy affecting me, even for just a moment, was that of insecurity and self-doubt, and it explained the tightness and confinement I felt en route.

I have met and worked with my fair share of individuals, each with their own distinct personality. I have come to find that I must be completely aware of any instantaneous feelings and emotions that come to me energetically when I walk into a new home, especially if the energetic awareness is disorderly and/or disruptive and influences me in any way. In this case, my uncustomary reaction of being conscious of my appearance as soon as I walked into Jasmine's home greatly aided me going into this session.

Jasmine opened the door to the laundry room and Billy and Lila, two rather large mix-breed dogs, came barreling out. The male had some Great Dane in him as did the female, which explained their girth and height. As they both ran toward me, Lila was looking to say hello first. However, before I knew it, Billy (who is larger than Lila) quietly sidled up to her and forcefully pushed her aside. He leaned into Lila and energetically whispered what I sensed to be a reminder to Lila of her hierarchical placement in the household order. Lila instantly slowed down, backed up, and let Billy push right into me to say hello as Lila waited to be second in line.

The look in Lila's eyes was distraught and full of anxiety. She demonstrated a closeted confusion that she had grown to accept. Clearly, Billy was the alpha, but he conducted his daily business with an underhanded energy. This was not the raw, organic, and natural energy typical of a healthy alpha. Billy was working with too much power. That power, although his to take as part of the alpha role, was, because of its excess, a foreign energetic substance attached to him that altered how alpha energy is normally distributed and expressed.

As Billy took his stance, Jasmine giggled and said, "He always does this. Lila knows he controls the house. I wish we could tone that down a bit because my husband encourages it. He got Billy before I came into the picture with Lila. It was pretty much this way or the highway."

I smiled and said, "Let's see what we can do. I would love to just observe Billy and Lila a bit before we really sit down and start seeing what the direct line of energy is."

Billy and Lila pounced in and out of the house. Yet every time they ran in or out, to the water bowl, to get a treat, or even to lie down, Billy was first in line. Interestingly enough, when I started to lock into the dogs' energy, I could see how Billy manipulated his alpha energy toward Lila. There was a silent yet stringent dictate he thrust upon her every moment, and Lila looked to unleash a little bit of freedom or perhaps lead her own direction. This excessive alpha energy shepherded Lila into an unhealthy family, home, and pack existence.

This is not to say that Billy, in any other household, wouldn't still command his natural innate alpha role. But, in this household, he has been given and has employed an additional wealth of human energetic neuroses, predominantly male, generating from a sense of human struggle occurring around him. The neuroses are a need for order and a need for dominance that have now crossed the line from natural to unnatural and unhealthy. This excessive alpha energetic vibration has spread like wildfire through the home, through Lila, and through Jasmine.

After completing my observations of Billy and Lila, I made the suggestion to begin introducing some quiet in the house, and to find a comfortable place for everyone to sit so we could get down to business. Clearly Jasmine made this appointment with every intention of not having her husband present. I see this a lot; most often in couples where one or the other (usually the non-dominant individual) requests to see me alone—on the sly so to speak. I make it a point to never question their decision or ask questions as to why they wanted to see me alone because I always discover the nature of the couple's relationship as the session progresses. And frankly, it is none of my business.

It was my business, role, and purpose in my session with Jasmine, Billy, and Lila to identify and assist in the removal of the unnatural excess alpha energy within the humans and animals so that a healthy and more balanced energy within and among them can return to everyone living in the household. It is up to the individuals who were present in the session to then do the work for themselves, their family, and their dogs. What information Jasmine chooses to convey and reveal to her husband remained to be seen.

Yet, in this moment, it was Jasmine who had the courage, wherewithal, and great desire to become open to something bigger in order to help herself, her dogs, and her home. For that I commended her. "I am proud of you for scheduling me here today. I know it was not easy to do." She smiled, looked down, and started to cry. We were ready to begin.

It was a struggle, to say the least, trying to get both Lila and Billy to sit with us comfortably and quietly on the floor. Whenever I addressed Jasmine or Lila, Billy slowly but forcefully pushed between us or blocked my view. Billy energetically communicated to me that he especially knew my mission and he wasn't exactly supportive of the change about to be instilled. He was not aggressive or out of control. Quite the opposite! He was precise, measured, and very controlled.

I noticed two crates in the kitchen that appeared to be in active use. Lila energetically communicated to me that she was often crated whenever Jasmine and her husband are not home, and on some days, just Lila was crated and not Billy. I asked Jasmine, "How are you keeping two very large dogs in crates all day?"

"Well," she said, "my husband doesn't trust Lila, primarily because she is prone to getting into mischief when we're gone."

"Exactly what happens when you don't cage the dogs when you leave?" I asked.

"Well, I don't really know because we have never left Lila out of her cage when we go. My husband just doesn't want to chance it."

I began getting down to business by focusing on Lila, who was being pushed away by Billy yet again. He dominated every inch of space that Lila tried to garner. I sternly communicated energetically to Billy and asked him for the space both Lila and I needed to accomplish the work that was to be done today—he acquiesced. I turned to Lila and looked into her eyes, and she was finally able to sit quietly next to me.

Since Billy was able to act on the energetic boundary I requested, it led me to believe that Billy had the potential to be the healthy alpha that was innate in him. At the same time, I understood that he also had the ability to discern the difference between natural leadership energy within the dog pack as opposed to taking on the human neuroses instigated by Jasmine's husband.

I detected that it was almost a relief to Billy that he was shown a way to go back, even for a moment, to his organic state of being. This did not come easily or consistently, mind you! Billy's alpha energy had been tarnished by Jasmine's husband's very strong human insecure need for control coupled with his underlying sense of fear—acquired traits that are completely unnatural for a true alpha.

With Lila and Billy quiet, I connected with both dogs to decipher their energy. In an interesting moment prior to this connection, Billy had energetically communicated to me that his alpha role occupied way too much of his time to the point where sometimes he acted outside his comfort zone as the alpha. Billy further communicated that he had taken too much power, and that Lila was literally drowning in it. It was clear to me that Lila had lost her identity and was desperately struggling to find her place within the home.

As I continued connecting with Lila and Billy, I sensed that Jasmine was getting very nervous as the dogs began releasing to me. When I asked if I could spend a few moments doing a little work on Lila before we went further, Jasmine sat back and reluctantly agreed. As I started to move energetically through Lila by lightly placing my hand on Lila's head, Billy jumped up and flew over to me like a bat out of hell. "Leave her alone," Billy energetically enforced as he pushed into me. Lila lowered her head and I felt this surge of emotion from her. She was trapped! While I was working on Lila, I could sense she was open to grow, expand, change, and move again with a natural course of energy. But with Billy's enforcement, the open energy flow had been stopped and Lila could no longer move naturally. The feeling that overcame me was that something had hold of her heart, her throat, and her soul. I felt very sick to my stomach and for a moment my head had pressure that literally stopped me in my tracks.

I looked up at Jasmine and said, "The alpha energy is too strong and too dominating. Between Billy and your husband, you and Lila couldn't possibly be living happily in this home. You are struggling to find your true path. Whenever you try to open up even slightly to find your purpose, you are stopped. The energy is so strong it has started to backfire onto you and Lila. Although you both seek alpha energy and could actually thrive from its direction, it has completely taken over. The weakest in the household are suffering tremendously, and both you and Lila are becoming very ill because of it.

"Jasmine, how often are you going to the doctor for one issue or another?" I noticed I struck a chord in her. As Jasmine's head dropped, so did Lila's. Jasmine started to stiffen, and her energy switched dramatically. I went too deep too fast. "You don't have to answer that," I said, "or speak about anything you don't want to. If I am wrong, by all means stop me. You see, sometimes I pick up another's energy through the dogs, and it may not be yours." Lila walked over to Jasmine, quietly leaned against Jasmine's legs, and looked up at Jasmine with very soft eyes. Jasmine lightly rubbed Lila's head as tears rolled down Jasmine's face.

"Yes," Jasmine said, "I have had many medical issues and feel like I am stuck in a world that isn't exactly working for me."

As Jasmine started to slowly open and become more outspoken, Billy sat up, walked over to her and Lila, and pushed Lila out of the way, appearing to remind both

Jasmine and Lila of Lila's place in the order of things. Billy was very serious about ending this process. Not only was he acting on what seemed to be his job, but he energetically let me know he was quite aware of what was going on, as if a vow of silence had just been broken. I was clearly a threat to the hierarchical order in place in the household.

While Billy was imposing his will, the air in the house seemed a little colder. Something definitely didn't want me there. When this occurs, I always try to take a new approach so that I can salvage the true purpose of the visit. We were not alone in the home. I sensed an attachment which plagued Jasmine. Almost like an "enforcer" attached to her that I sensed she had picked up a couple of years prior. This attachment functioned between both Jasmine and Lila, which I found very interesting. An attachment is an energy or spirit that attaches to humans. Some people can have up to twenty different attachments, or some can have just one attachment with the force of twenty. The latter was the case here.

Jasmine and I sat in silence for a few moments. A very strong ego energy had taken over, was working against me, and attempting to push me out of the house. Within that silence, I decided to remove the attachment from and between Jasmine and Lila. As I was moving energy and asking the dark energetic presence to leave, I never uttered a word. I worked completely internally, never alerting the dogs and, most importantly, not alarming Jasmine. All of a sudden I saw the dark energy move out, adhering to my request.

Immediately, the overall energy in the room shifted. Even though we sat in a very uncomfortable silence, I reminded myself that I was there for a reason. I knew I was certainly not very popular in that room at that moment, but I was determined to prevail in helping this family. Plus, being the most unpopular in a room when working to take ownership is something I am used to. Believe me! Taking ownership is a very difficult message to deliver, and thus I am not everyone's favorite.

With the change in energy, you could instantly tell Jasmine, Lila, and even Billy felt a lift. Jasmine's eyes raised and looked at me with a softness, an openness.

"Do you think Lila feels that she needs freedom?" Jasmine asked.

I paused for a moment and quietly said, "Yes." I made it very clear. "Billy is an alpha. That is his natural leadership role. Your husband has a real need to harness control based on his insecurity, and to dominate the household, particularly you and Lila. That is his dominant role and his neurosis. This neurosis in turn has harnessed the two submissive female energies within the household—you and Lila. Your husband's compelling need has energetically drenched Billy's mind and is very powerful. But this kind of power is not clean because its core is gripped with your husband's lack of self-worth. When this occurs, the dominant looks for any outside source to attach to in order to gain the control he or she needs. His struggle has reached such a high octane level energetically that it is fueling Billy in a very neurotic and unhealthy way. Your husband has corrupted an already dominant source in Billy, resulting in a disruption of the natural alpha energy that should be flowing through Billy and throughout the household, but is not."

Jasmine sat and listened as her eyes dropped to the floor. The struggle within her was now front and center. Jasmine started to take ownership and acknowledged, "You know, nothing in this house is mine. I feel like a prisoner sometimes. If I stray from the standard protocol, order is enforced. I don't know who I am anymore, what I want, or where I want to go in my life. It's as if I am stuck in this bubble with no life force to breathe."

"You are stuck in a bubble," I agreed. "The life force energy that once moved freely has now stopped to the point where no one is growing anymore, including you, Lila, Billy, and your husband."

It was time to focus again on Lila. "Let's discuss Lila's connection to you and this disruption," I encouraged. "You are forcing Lila to be crated literally every moment you are not present. You haven't tried to even slowly integrate her into the home, to socialize on her own with Billy, or make any free choices. In fact, you don't even know what her general reaction would be if she were able to make some of her own decisions without anyone else involved. I, of course, am not telling you to let her run amuck. Yet, the energy circle in the home needs to be altered drastically."

"How do I do that," Jasmine asked, "because I'm not getting much support from Billy or my husband, and I feel as if I couldn't even possibly find the means within me to do that!"

"One thing you need to know," I said, "is that Lila came to you for a reason and vice versa. Lila has the same personality as you and somewhat the same history. It is karma for both you and Lila to travel with the issue of maintaining your own space within a healthy environment. You each struggle with a confidence issue, yours stemming from your mother. Each of you has been content to hold on to those issues for quite some time. That is, until now. And now, the test really begins."

I continued. "We come to certain times in our lives when change must occur to learn the lessons we are supposed to learn in a given lifetime. When the energy we have been working with starts to turn dark, it is no different than having a toothache that you ignore for a long time until you don't feel it anymore. We convince ourselves that when the ache isn't present, then we must not have an obstruction. Well, as you and I know, that is never the case. Months, even years pass, and that toothache turns into a root canal, and if it's not taken care of, the tooth will completely die. When you finally get around to handling it, you could lose the whole tooth because of your own neglect and denial. I use this example because it is one I know very well!"

Jasmine laughed and then said, "Then I may need a few teeth pulled at this point!" We both laughed.

I made it clear that Lila must know how to function in a world where she has the freedom to move and make choices without being regulated every single moment. She didn't want to be caged unnecessarily. I could see that unless the necessary changes were made and the household energy became more balanced, Jasmine will continue to have health problems and Lila's digestive system will start to shut down. Lila, Jasmine, and Billy needed to change their situation immediately before they became suffocated by their own energy. And because we didn't have the husband present that day, we had to make those changes without him.

Ultimately, clearing an energetic disturbance when the source is not present at the time of the session, although more difficult, can still be successful if the individuals who are there, and who are disrupted by it, stand up, take ownership, and say, " I am ready to get my life and my dogs' lives healthy now." I knew that changing this dominant energy would open up energetic portals previously unavailable to them. I have found that one glimpse of light and a chance to take a clear new breath are very powerful and will always triumph over stagnant, controlled, dark energy.

I asked Jasmine to sit on the floor with me, Billy, and Lila. I began working on Billy first. I moved to Billy's head and lightly put my hand on it. I worked immediately to remove the energetic hold placed on Billy by his master and human companion. Their energies were as intricately intertwined as I thought. In fact, as I quietly worked, Billy finally energetically revealed to me that he constantly waited for any vibration from Jasmine's husband even when he wasn't present. Billy was so strongly connected to Jasmine's husband that I sensed Billy could feel him throughout the day when he tightened up at work, got frustrated, or struggled with control—all of this on a very subliminal energetic level.

I knew that Billy wanted to be the alpha, but he had lost his lead. Although he loved Lila and Jasmine, he had lost the ability to appreciate or enjoy those loving moments with either of them. He was angry and that anger was not his own. Funny thing, Billy communicated to me that he had reached out to Jasmine energetically to help him find some clear direction, but she either didn't pick up his energy or she didn't want to listen. I believe this was because

Jasmine had anger toward both Billy and her husband, and unconsciously identified Billy's actions as her husband's. Jasmine had been repelled by Billy and could not look at Billy as the innocent bystander that he was. Therefore, Jasmine's only response to Billy, when Billy looked for some guidance from her, was that of resentment.

I continued to work on Billy with both hands to energetically move out the neuroses attached to him so he could return to a healthy alpha energy state. I discovered that Billy was willing to let go of some issues, and for others he was confused. Billy frantically moved his head to get my hands off of him. He knew exactly what I was doing. Just as a human finds it difficult to let go of core issues they have carried for years or maybe even since birth, a dog that has been conditioned by and immersed in a human companion's neuroses is also frightened to walk in any other light.

The more I worked on Billy, the more he let go. He closed his eyes, spread his legs out nice and long (not short and stiff), and let out a sigh, a release. For those moments, Billy had broken free from the human control and direction enforced upon him. When I finished with Billy, he started to take a little nap. He rested with a clear mind, probably for the first time in quite a while.

I came to the conclusion that Billy was a really good dog with wonderful intentions who truly loved both Lila and Jasmine. With Billy released, I finally had the chance to also move Lila and Jasmine into a healthy clear light. "Jasmine," I said, "Lila is your mirror image. Moving forward, whenever you are not aware of your energetic connection to yourself or you feel thrown off, it will most notably reflect in Lila. It is very important for you to be aware of what it feels like, right in this moment, to be connected to yourself, Lila, Billy, and your home. Doing this daily, even for a few minutes, is essential to maintaining that connection and awareness. It is the key to all of this. If you are not increasingly aware at every moment of yourself, your environment, and what you project energetically, than none of this will work.

"Your brain is a very powerful source, one that can make or break your soul connection. If you focus your mind's energy in a healthy way, and don't hold on to ungrounded untruthful emotions, you won't be thrown off track. Once you take ownership of your unhealthy core issues and work on removing the dark, static, negative energies generated by them, the real 'mind surgery' occurs. Just as when you come home from the hospital after major medical surgery, you must take precaution in how you recover and heal from this removal process as well. In order not to return to an unhealthy state of mind, remember to be highly aware of being kind to yourself, and of caring for the way you heal. Once I leave, the work you do is imperative in order to nurture yourself and correctly move forward."

Jasmine looked scared. "Can I really do this without your instructing me? I feel nervous."

I assured her that she had already made a tremendous contribution in getting us to this point. "If you were not completely on board mentally and energetically to begin with," I said, "I would have left a couple of hours ago because it would have meant you weren't ready. That clearly wasn't the case. You did this on your own, I only helped the process. You need to hold to this moment and the changes you so readily want. Our minds and the vibrations we create are all our own doing—you must always know that. How we let someone contribute to it or fuel what we created is our choice. Seeing and feeling light is wonderful. The problem is we are too often more comfortable with the darker energy even if it kills us!"

It was time to give Jasmine some instruction. "For five minutes a day, I would like you to put yourself in a quiet space. It doesn't matter whether you stand or sit; just close your eyes, take some deep breaths, and ask the Universe for balance, protection, and the ability to move forward with a clear aware mind. Actually see what you *want*. See your breath as a flow of sheer light; send that light to any place you may need it, and direct how and where you want to distribute it. Then ask to be grounded and rooted, and send energy from the Universe down through your body, down to your feet and into the earth. Once that happens, release the given energy back out through your crown chakra (the head), and return it to the Universe.

"Once you are done, I want you to say 'Thank You!' Thank you is so important. Being gracious in life is important, and it begins with you. It is pivotal to thank the Universe for the connection and protection you need in order to do your work to change your energy. Let it become a mantra. This daily mantra, along with clearing and moving your energy, will inevitably keep you aware, connected, and in tune. Then your outward vibration will slowly change all the energy around you. What you vibrate out will return to you to benefit your journey. Then Lila and Billy will have the strength and ability to grow into a healthy state within a healthy environment, and will wholeheartedly support the great change you are beginning to instill."

Jasmine slowly petted Lila's head, and then quietly, and right in front of me, without my even asking, went into the energetic connection mantra I had given her. I smiled as she closed her eyes and went into it. Lila's tail started to wag. As Jasmine's eyes were closed, I watched two of her guides stand beside her. Lila and I could see energy moving all over the place! I was pleased to say the least.

When Jasmine was done she said, "How did I do? I feel really nice. Wow! That felt like such a short period of time. Can I go longer?"

"Absolutely," I said. "I just didn't want to overwhelm you because moderation is so important. Life is filled with extremes, and we can't get much accomplished if we don't at least find a happy medium. This filters out to every aspect of our lives, but it's especially true when changing an energetic path. Do whatever feels right."

At this point, we all stood up and I gave everyone a very big hug. As we started to walk out, I saw Lila run to the water bowl for a drink. Billy just hung out next to me and let Lila move unrestrained. Jasmine smiled. When we ended the session, Jasmine handed me a piece of cake she had baked earlier as a snack for my long ride home. The air in the home was different, light and reflective.

I felt comfortable leaving Jasmine, Lila, and Billy to continue on the road less traveled, on a journey that will open them up to a world in which they can live freely. An alpha energy had been restored to a healthier state. Jasmine had committed to take a leap of faith, and to give herself and her dogs a chance to feel the energetic circumference that encourages rather than hinders. They were beginning a journey that promised hope, balance, and a healthier energetic landscape. My hope was that this new journey would also include Jasmine's husband. Again, that remained to be seen.

I thought it ironic that Jasmine was wearing yellow from head to toe. Without her knowledge, she was already in transition, looking for renewal and a higher psychic connection.

When I turned to get into my car, I glanced back at Jasmine standing in the doorway. She was radiating light. That same light wrapped around Lila and Billy. It was beautiful and effervescent. A new day had begun.

The Natural Pack

The way it's supposed to work in nature is that the alpha (either male or female) is the leader in the dog pack to which other members of the pack are submissive. The order from the alpha down to the submissives is known and understood by all the pack animals. The alpha dog is confident and maintains control, and those dogs that adopt this role adopt it instinctually. They don't act above and beyond what is known innately.

In a natural pack, the alpha is not neurotically obsessing over the control of every moment or everyone in the pack. In the case of a male alpha, if the females of the group want to move, get a drink of water, or socialize with certain members of the pack, the alpha does not need to always move in to stop their behavior or block their actions. This is not to say that the alpha does not instigate order, but if so instigated, the movement is precise and unobstructed, and used only when absolutely necessary.

Then who really *is* the alpha? Well, I believe the game plan has changed quite a bit, and we need to look closely at re-examining all the sources that contribute to alpha energy in the human-dog world.

I have found that most often the role adopted by the alpha dog in a home is very different from the traditional role played by the alpha dog within a pack. In a pack of dogs or, taken a step further, in a wolf pack mentality, there can be shifts in the alpha position. Sometimes a shift is easy and sometimes it necessitates battle to establish the leadership role. Once the battles are over, the alpha leadership decision is made and worked through. The pack understands that it must adhere and submit to the alpha leadership decision, and then they all go back to living in a natural flow of energy within the raw organic state that existed prior to the shift in alpha position. All of this occurs, of course, without human intervention.

Within a household of more than one dog, however, I find that the alpha remains the alpha although sometimes there can be a switch of position. Now add to the mix a strong dominant human supplying the alpha dog with insecurity and excessive control and your end result is an unstable mass of energy where the fine line between natural order and unnatural order can be crossed in an instant. Once crossed, coupled with a long duration of unnatural behavior from both animal and human, the repercussions within the household become so chaotic as to be virtually irreversible. Animals get confused and out of energetic balance when humans get involved irresponsibly. The ramifications are more overwhelming than we really know! Now the question is, what does one do about changing the tarnished alpha energy within a modern day household?

If you have an alpha and a submissive in both animal and human form within an unhealthy household, the submissives suffer energetically just as much as the alphas. Let's break this down even further.

An emitted energetic vibration within an environment affects everyone, and when it is unnatural or toxic, it causes a disruption. Energy vibrations exist in a vast circle of energy that affect every single living breathing soul that circle encompasses. One energetic vibration leads to another, and where there is weakness within the circle, the weak link will be monumentally affected. In the human-dog world, since humans are perceived to carry the dominant energetic gene over the "weaker" dog (which is unfortunate but true), I strongly believe that the real, energetic, vibrational change must start with humans. Case closed.

We all know you cannot take a pill and and have your life instantly change. Energetic vibrational change is work, dedication, and a concentrated process for all involved, but once the process has started, the healthier journey is well worth taking. The responsibility must be ours to be aware and conscious of maintaining a clear healthy state of mind and staying within that light. We humans owe it to ourselves, our animals, the ones that love us, and the ones that surround us to produce a healthier energetic environment.

Now that we have broken down the properties of vibrational energy, how it moves and can be changed, we can better appreciate the interwoven energies between human and animal (alphas and submissives) within the household. Once the dominant human relinquishes control and opens to switching her own and her environmental energy, then she must stay the course and next enforce energetic boundaries upon the household and its animals with a calm, even, and neutral delivery.

As boundaries are enforced upon the alpha, a natural energetic progression takes place. Giving the alpha the upper hand in various situations in multiple-dog households creates this natural energetic flow throughout the home. It's palpable. For example, we get the alpha leashed up for a walk first, and give food to the alpha first. After we tend to the alpha, we immediately do the same for the other dogs. When we do this, the alpha moves more naturally within the household to enforce order. Everyone needs to know that the alpha is the alpha. When the alpha is done eating, quietly use your energy to enforce that the alpha not leave its food and go steal from the others. Also, discourage any overly aggressive behavior from the alpha, such as jumping on tables or lashing out when feeling threatened.

This goes hand-in-hand with human behavior. As you quietly and energetically enforce boundaries upon your animals, those same energetic boundaries must be enforced within yourself and your household. The change of energy flow within you and your household, your animals, and particularly within the alpha, does not change the hierarchical position of the alpha (human or dog) or the submissives (human or dog) within the home—it simply gives birth to an energetic balance. To be clear, I am not trying to debunk any current alpha or pack leader theories within the animal world. I just think it is time to re-examine those theories to broaden our points of view by including the existence, awareness, and effects of the interconnecting and contributing energies of everyone in the household, not just the alpha and the submissives.

The potential for how we can better communicate within ourselves and with our animals is extraordinary. We can be the pack leader but not a dictator; we can be a submissive but not a pushover. To allow free thought, neutral stable movement, moderation, and the ability to feel secure in turn creates a healthy happy household. When energy is redirected in these ways, the rewards for us all, human and animal, are to truly enjoy who we are, and to appreciate who we are to each other.

Even the alpha theories we are re-examining can be better appreciated–they are not mutually exclusive. In the final analysis, does the alpha "dog" in the household solely derive its power and dominance from the innate and natural characteristic of leadership that controls the pack in the wild, with all the other pack members being naturally submissive to the alpha? If yes, this is the simple, current, and traditional model. Or, as I see it, does the alpha "dog" in the present-day more complicated human-dog household derive its power and dominance not only from the innate and natural characteristic of leadership, but also from additional contributing factors coming from a multiple source of animal and human energies that live and exist within the household? Those energies are innate and natural as well as extrinsic, reactionary, and unnatural, and are energetically connected to each other in a manner that has been completely ignored.

I have found that the best way to answer such important questions is not in the form of a detached scientific theory, but rather by looking deeply into ourselves and to our own everyday experiences with our family dogs to discover such wisdom.

Chapter Seven

Rescue Animals and What They Inherit

I want to share an example where no matter what I do or how long I stay, if a human being will not be open to the process, then the dog, as well as the human companion, will not be released from his current state of mind. The story of Ben, a dog rescued by a husband and wife, illustrates this type of struggle.

Ben

In this particular case, the human companion was too immersed in ego and held on to his conditioned state of mind. He held on so tightly, fighting and resisting, that it was destroying a dog's mind that was already in decline from its previous family. He had so many serious issues of fear and insecurity that he was scared of me. He knew what I was there to do, and yet he didn't know how to live without his fear and insecurity. And that wasn't the animal—I am referring to the human companion.

Whenever I get a call or email, even when I stay neutral, I instantly start feeling the issues that are in play. In this case, I got an email from a woman who had a dog that she and her husband rescued. She believed the dog came from a situation where there had been some abuse, and that he had many serious neuroses. She had already given me too much information. Anytime I speak with a potential client, I don't want to know more than the dog's name. I could already tell she was hoping I would work with her and that if she laid it all on the table, maybe I would spend some time with them.

I will be honest. I was very hesitant. And, it wasn't because of her; it was because of her husband. I felt his energy instantly. As much as I want to help the animal, and as protected as I am, the process can drain my energy when there is such deep resistance from the human whose soul is fighting me. No matter what assistance I call in from my Guides, when it is very dark and challenging, it is almost best to bless the individual and move on until they are no longer resistant and are receptive.

The particular guides that protect me and help me guard against these kinds of dark and challenging forces are very sacred to me. I am often asked, "Who are these guides, what do they look like, and what do they say to you?" It is against my practice and what I believe in to reveal with any specificity what these guides look like and what they say to me. But what I can tell you the following: they are in human form, they are ancient, they have been with me for many lifetimes, and they only speak and reveal themselves to me. As I would never ask for anyone to reveal what they see and speak to personally on a spiritual level that is sacred to them, I cannot reveal mine.

We all must keep very close to us anything that comes to us to lend a hand, whether it is metaphysical, spiritual, religious, or whatever you believe in and in whatever form it comes to you. It must remain with you only, for that is when it has its most powerful effect. I don't need to know, friends don't need to know, and even your animal doesn't need to know . . . although it already does. We all too often feel as if we need to tell everything, and we must answer every question. I am here to tell you that this is a Universe. It is very large and very expansive. When dealing in metaphysics, sometimes things just cannot be explained. We must take back what is sacred and what cannot be explained, nor should it. It is like asking someone kneeling at an altar to tell you their private conversations with God.

Forcing the process when there is deep resistance can, at times, do more detriment to me, and then no one comes out for the better. This was one of those cases. Betty contacted me. She was desperate. I accepted.

I knocked on the door and, frankly, immediately wanted to turn around. As beautiful as I want this process to be, even though I can deliver and work with energy on a high level, it can also be quite brutal. That is because I am human. So despite the neutrality I adopt, I can't deny the intuition upon which my life is based. That intuition suggested to me that no matter what I did, this was an unhealthy environment. And, you cannot make it healthy. I must admit—I pushed my intuition aside and walked into the house.

Ben was upstairs barking a nervous bark that wasn't his own. I walked in and saw Ben on the second level of the stairs barking in a tight circle. His eyes were glazed over as if his soul was so long gone he would not even recognize it if it was retrieved. That is, unless everyone in the household fully supported it. Betty asked, "Do you want me to drag him down?" and I told her absolutely not. I insisted that we not force anything. I told her I would just sit quietly right below the stairs, and let Ben understand who I am and that I was not going to force anything on him. Unfortunately, Ben acted out erratically and ran upstairs into a little room on the corner of a hallway. By this point in time, I had been there for fifteen minutes.

Ben was acting out of a type of hypnosis that was entirely humanly instigated. It was the same as an emotionally battered woman, child, or man who is defending their abuser. A type of mind control that, in this case, was coming from one of the companions who was using the severe weakness of an animal with a history of abuse so that the animal could worship and cater to the vast insecurity and dominance that was within that human companion. It was quite a sick game—one that ultimately had one significant loser—the dog. The dog had no chance to get out of this state because he had been pulled too far out of his true nature. It was as if the dog couldn't function unless the human companion's energy dictated the dog's every move.

I see this far more often than I would like. It is hard enough to watch when it is the treatment of one human being to another, but it is even more devastating from a human to a dog because the human knows they can do it, and they justify it. "He loves me and needs me." With an animal, they are destitute until the day they die, and as long as it continues, they live in darkness with a mind full of mental disease.

I asked Betty, "Who is upstairs? Is it your husband?" Betty said, "Yes. Ben loves Bob. Ben is just protecting him. When people come in, Ben constantly does this running and barking, and rushes to Bob." I slightly smiled and said, "Well, I have been here for about twenty minutes at this point. Why hasn't Bob brought the dog downstairs to join us? He knew I was coming, right?" With apprehension, Betty replied, "Yes."

I then turned directly to Betty and said, "Well, I know Bob doesn't remotely want me here and he is issuing his dominance over me by controlling the dog to stay with him. Quite frankly, this is not going to help the situation for which you hired me. He is generally toying with me because deep inside your husband knows I want to change the situation you have here, and that is the last thing he wants."

Betty said quietly that I was right, and that Bob didn't think it was necessary for me to be there. But, as she put it, he would "humor" me.

I kept myself continually neutral when all I wanted to really do was go upstairs to that man, let him know his little antics were not going over well with me, leash up the dog, and get it out of that house. I am sure that wouldn't have been very humorous to him.

It was the health and wellbeing of the dog that mattered here. If I was going to open up this process, I needed the man upstairs to come downstairs and out of his "zone" with the animal. I asked Betty to please call Bob and ask him to come downstairs and bring Ben with him. Betty called twice. Then Bob finally answered that he would be down. I smiled and continued to wait. Contrary to her husband, Betty was open to the process and really wanted to help Ben. She loved him, and Ben was "the family dog."

Bob walked down the stairs with Ben right at his side. Bob was about 5'10," approximately 285 pounds, a big man. He had cold eyes, and behind those eyes was a voice that said, when he looked at me, "You will never break what I have with this dog. I own him. He is mine. I tell him what to do, what to feel, and where to go. I feed his already tortured mind and we are happy this way. Now back off."

"Hi, I'm Jocelyn. It's so nice to meet you" I said, and extended my hand. He barely shook it, and sat on the sofa.

Not knowing why he was doing it, Ben did not stop barking and running around. His eyes were still glazed over. He then jumped up on the sofa right next to Bob. As I sat on the floor between Betty and Bob, Ben stared at me. The energy was so overwhelming that I had to close my eyes for a moment. I don't normally do this unless I have already come into contact with the dog. Even then, it is just for a few moments to make the connection and do what I need to. Ben looked at me and as he was barking, I could feel Bob's energy and thoughts saying, "Good boy. She isn't going to change you."

With every determined stroke by Bob on Ben's head, Ben's voice would get louder, his eyes would roll all around, his head would twitch, and I could sense he felt disoriented. Without even touching him, I tried to connect with Ben and I heard a faint voice saying, "Please help me." I knew I didn't necessarily need to retrieve either of the human souls but to gain a feel for Ben's soul. I needed that to try to bridge the gap between Ben and me.

I asked several of my Guides to come in and force a link between us. Once I got that, I determined that Ben had indeed come from abuse before this family adopted him. He experienced actual physical as well as mental abuse. He was locked up for long periods of time, sometimes by chain and sometimes in a dark room. Food and water were scarce, and I believe he witnessed the beatings of his sisters and brothers as well. A male human being had control from the beginning. Ben probably was removed from his former home, and then adopted by Betty and Bob. Although Ben is in this beautiful home where no one ever harms him physically, he is still caught in an emotional mudslide. Bob is well aware of that.

This is a beautiful dog, a large mutt with a gorgeous coat that really loves his home and his human companions, and outwardly gets treated with care. He is given all the necessities and is well fed. This was never in question. However, all this in the end means nothing because his mind is still in the same place as if someone were beating him. Ben cannot possibly understand the way he is treated because he is nowhere near being "in the moment," nowhere near a natural light, and is so tormented mentally he cannot possibly enjoy the gifts around him.

I went over and sat next to Ben. I asked Bob to move to another chair and not to hover over him. Eventually, Ben started to respond to my energy, to release, and allow me to connect all the energy of the house, Bob and Betty, and then move the energy right back to Ben.

Through this process, I learned that when Bob isn't home, Ben is able to relax more with Betty, and that Betty doesn't enforce any neurotic hold on Ben's mind. Because Betty works at home, people come in and out of the house. Although Ben barks at them, Betty's energy puts no emphasis on it. Therefore, Ben doesn't feel a need to become anxious and torment himself. He is temporarily able to enjoy another's company and feels a bit more at ease. Unfortunately, Bob is never far behind because his business also keeps him home most of the time.

As soon as Bob makes his presence known, it is as if there is a mechanism triggered in Ben's mind that sends him under a control he doesn't understand. When Bob takes him to the dog park, for example, Ben has incredible difficulties functioning among the other dogs. He is pushy and aggressive. Then, he becomes very passive, running from them and not knowing how to just be. Ben doesn't have any understanding of the other dogs because his mind is fully controlled by Bob's energy that is saying to Ben: "You must need me, and only me. I am the only thing that matters. All your anxieties are reinforced by me. So, go ahead and be confused. The more confused you are, the stronger I think I am."

The odd thing is, while my energy was circulating through Ben and I was making some headway, I noticed Bob ever so quietly snapping his fingers at his side for the dog to look at him. As soon as he looked at Bob, Ben started to quietly growl at me. Then he quickly got up and started a barking tirade while he circled Bob. Bob giggled and laughed, and let me know in a condescending voice that he "wasn't doing anything."

Before I could speak, Betty forcefully interrupted and told Bob to stop it. She told him we are never going to get anywhere if he doesn't cooperate. Bob said he didn't do anything. Yet, Betty and I both witnessed otherwise. She was starting to lose patience with him. When Bob is in the room, it is as if Betty doesn't even exist for Ben. She needed to regain control. As I retrieved her soul on a personal level so she could truly see the light of the moment, she got stronger and stronger and more insistent that Bob cooperate. Her eyes were brighter and her energy became clearer. She could see that her husband was prohibiting the mental health of the dog she loved so much.

I turned to Bob and asked if I could be candid with him. He nodded reluctantly, and I told him exactly what I was getting from the energy in the household. "You are controlling what you know to be the weak and dependent mind of this dog. When Betty calls him over or tries to spend time with Ben and you are present, the dog looks to you to see if he can go over to her or not. You are more than aware that Ben is lost and bewildered, and you have taken full advantage of that. I see you giggle when this behavior comes out.

"When I arrived, I could feel your energy and what your motivations are with respect to me, Ben, and this process. Those motivations are not too far from how you are on a day-to-day basis. It is not fair to Betty or to you, and most importantly, it is unfair to Ben.

"Where you think Ben fully loves you and is dedicated to you, he is actually sending energy that conflicts with what you are sending. He can't possibly know what it truly feels like to trust and love you because a part of him, and what guides him, is well aware of the agenda you possess. When there is an agenda, there can't possibly be any clarity. Under those circumstances, this dog couldn't find the light if it was shined right in his eyes, and he has no chance to be in the moment. So the love or devotion you feel from Ben and the power you feel over Ben is basically a working illusion. The only one that truly believes they exist is you. That is the problem.

"The way you touch him, and your thoughts while you are alone or with others, are all very dark, tainted, and destructive. You seem to be at a time in your life where you feel somewhat lost, useless, and insecure. You have lost your identity, and your self-esteem is not what it used to be. You work sparingly, and your wife works all the time. You have lost faith in yourself. You long for serious control. You want something that your mind, your energy, and your voice can control to the fullest, almost to the point that if you could form your own little cult, you would." Surprisingly, Bob grinned ever so slightly. He was indeed caught! I joked with him saying that if he moved to some vast open land in a remote section of Texas, then he could definitely get a little "organization" going on his own.

I told him he couldn't possibly be happy with the situation in his home, or with the state of his mind. Most importantly, I knew he loved Ben. Knowing that, how could he possibly be happy with the condition in which Ben was living? Giving Ben back his original soul and light would be such a gift, and would let Ben know what it feels like to live in that moment. However, the problem was that all of Ben's and my energy would be wasted if I brought Ben into that light because I knew as soon as I left, Bob would instantly resume his mind control over Ben.

Ben is very, very fragile and not the usual dog. Once the soul retrieval occurs, even if the human companion is slow to accept it, the dog usually can stay within it and start adjusting instantly to support his own true nature. With Ben, that would not be the case. Ben's soul retrieval would *have* to be supported. Knowing that it wouldn't be, I was hesitant to give Ben his moment because it would be unfair to him.

Bob then made me aware of some of the mind control sessions he had with a few individuals. In my opinion, those individuals claim to have a "spiritual nature," they charge a lot of money, bring everyone together for a few days, and soak their minds with what is meant to be very confusing and disorienting information. They perform rituals that are very dark, even involving calling up the dead, and they are at the radical end of what they believe is the spectrum of "light and love."

Let me say this. I have a lot of knowledge of many beliefs and practices. I have worked with many individuals who are real masters and servants of a higher nature. The one thing I know and have learned is that you have to be very careful when calling dark forces into your life to aid or help you with anything. That is why they are called dark forces, folks. What people do on their own time is their own process. As long as it doesn't hurt or affect others in a negative way, then who am I, or anyone for that matter, to say what to do or not do? It is when the individuals leading the program are not fully educated that the dark energy being brought from it travels with you and can be destructive beyond comprehension.

The situation I found myself in at this home was clearly that case. Bob was using much of what he learned from those types of individuals in those kinds of settings, in addition to the energy that already traveled with him, to make Ben a servant to the dark mind.

Let me give you an idea of the workshops Bob was attending and what he was practicing to explain how destructive such spiritual work *can* be. I stress the word "can" because when you engage in spiritual practices like this without proper energetic protection, without full knowledge of what energies you are calling in and why, and without a human guide to properly lead you, the repercussions to your energetic space are enormous. These programs come in all forms and can be called many things. Bob said they were advertised as "bringing in the dark, to find the light." Hmmm . . . a bit vague. I wondered about that concept because unless you truly understand spirituality, higher energetic frequencies, and various Shamanic practices, it is dangerous to usher in dark energies through the "lower region" which is the frequency that allows you to travel to where the dark resides. Getting to the darkness isn't always the issue, but getting out is! Having allowed the darkness to connect and attach to your energy, we are then to believe you are instantaneously returned to the light! This is especially troublesome as Bob said he had no idea of anything metaphysical until he signed up for the workshop.

Through long hours of process and meetings, Bob said the key was to balance the dark energy brought in by various dark spirits or "beasts" with the light of your own life. This is done through offerings, prayer, and chanting. "The two coming together forms real power going forward," he said. I stared at Bob for a good sixty seconds just to take a breath and to think how I should respond. I asked twice for Bob to explain this to me, if he thought he found the balance he was seeking, and whether these sessions actually created some progress in his life. He responded, "I don't know how to use what I learned, but I know I am accessing some strong dark forces in my everyday life. I also believe that Ben is actually benefiting more than anyone!"

I looked over at Ben who is riddled with more dark attachments than I have ever seen on any animal in my life. His eyes were full of terror! At this point, the only person who is "benefitting" is Bob, and given that he doesn't even know how he is benefitting, it is safe to say *no one* is!

This was very difficult for me. Unless I pulled that dog growling and barking out of the house while the human companions called the cops on me, there wasn't a lot I could do in a couple of hours in their home. As much as Betty reprimanded Bob and told him to please stop doing what he was doing, I knew he wouldn't stop.

So I accepted what I knew and identified various health issues with the animal. These generally had to do with anxiety and abandonment. I went over some nice herbal remedies with Betty that could help Ben quiet down. When other individuals came into the house, I recommended the best method to quiet Ben, and how Betty could switch her energy to do that. I told Betty that she had to go into a quiet state, almost like a pre-meditative state, a place between going into meditation and preparing the body for meditation. Then I told her to change her breathing, start breathing slowly, feet placed on the ground, connected to the Earth, and ask to be released from the chaotic energy into a neutral state. Each breath taken after that was to be taken with neutrality. I asked her to visualize her breath in any way that was suitable to her in a clear light. I wanted her to see her breath in a clear neutral state, however she wanted to do that. Then, she needed to ask for that neutral calm state to be radiated out into the home, and specifically ask that all of her intentions and energy be focused on Ben to have his energy cleared. Once she had dedicated that, I told her to hold that intention within the fresh breath created from when she was clearing, and when she released that breath out, that would be the final intention of her new energetic state—and to not let that go.

I then tried to do my own work with Ben regarding trust and quiet by walking through the house and switching my energy from static to neutral, with the same methods I explained to Betty, so that Ben could start understanding the difference. In this way, I tried to impart to him that instead of barking and growling at everything, he actually had some movement with his energy and could have "moments" of being in his true nature where he could respond when it was warranted and not respond when it was not.

Ben started to trust me and sense that I was educating him on where his true light is, and where it is not. I spent a while doing this and could see that he was happy to understand it. Every time I would stop moving or quizzing him, he asked for me to continue, and so I did. This trust allowed me to sit next to him and do some serious cranial energy work. I tried to really remove as much fear as I could from Ben—to look for his original soul and bring it back, to give it my best shot, and bring some peace into his life. Once I did that, I protected Ben with energy like he was Fort Knox! Ben was in heaven. He looked up at me when I was done and had a peace like he had just run a marathon and this was his first break to relax. His head fell into my hands and his eyes were no longer glazed over or confused. He was basking in a light he didn't even know existed.

When I stepped away, I kept Ben's serenity to myself as I knew this would probably not last because Bob was not going to comply. Unfortunately, Ben wasn't strong enough yet to get there on his own. I did the best I could, and sent a force of energy through Ben that I rarely send through an animal. Something I don't always do unless it's a very hard case.

When I left, I hoped my work would endure and rise above the darker energy, which I asked to leave both the house and the family, and to stay away. When I walked out the door, I got in my car and cried. This was one of those times I knew I needed the strength to disconnect, and accept that I may not have succeeded as I had hoped.

Because they are animals and not human beings doesn't mean dogs shouldn't be treated with the same respect we humans demand. This was so much the case with Ben and Bob. We need outlets that allow us to feel certain things, and we need to do things we enjoy. Sometimes your animal stays home for those moments, and sometimes they don't. You can both have your own identities and enjoy the same or different things as well. That sounds like a fairly healthy relationship to me. One that can do wonders for you and your pet in your everyday lives.

Let us remember that animals live in the moment and are so grateful for our kindness. They see so much good even when, as with so many rescues, they are scared or have been battered. They don't have masks. They don't plan or devise. They can be great manipulators if they want to, and I smile as I say this, yet overall their minds are pure. They are all of a great spiritual nature and have, without ego, taken the role in society that human beings have placed on them. Let us choose carefully what role that should be, and what they should inherit.

When I am asked what the hardest situation is that I have dealt with, it will always be, without a doubt, a dog struggling with a complete loss of identity and a human companion with the exact same condition. The companion has usually showered the animal with every possible neurosis. The dog is pulled into being a part of one of the identities the human being wants to preserve, and the companion literally orders or commands the dog to be what the companion thinks she needs. It is usually very forceful, very needy, and extremely serious. Humans can function like this for years, not even really knowing if this is the right way to live, and continually tell the animal to support it. The saddest part of this charade is if the animal has come to the human companion entirely different from what is needed to support the companion's neurosis, then the animal's identity crisis starts forming the instant they come into the human's life. The animal becomes the enabler without choice.

Rescue dogs get this a lot in many different forms. One example is the potential companion who hasn't had a relationship, a real friendship, or much socialization. When the human goes to adopt a dog, believe it or not, as they look over and identify the available dogs, their conditioned mind looks for what appears to be the most willing participant to enable their conditioned lifestyle. They want it. They need it. And, what better way to "feel" like you are taking the initiative to better and share your life with something than by getting a dog?

Where you are in your life generally tends to determine what you are looking for in an animal. If you are looking to keep yourself in full isolation with every neurosis powered on all cylinders, then you will look for an animal that you neatly feel will accommodate that. You may look for one that is older, usually with some kind of issue, that keeps it inside as often as possible, and one that looks like it will never get adopted . . . that's when you smile and say, "I will take that one!"

The animal might also be like your boyfriend, husband, friend, or therapist, and you will condition and teach it how to function like that for you. You strip the dog of all its identity so it can become yours, become a mini-you. You can still stay inside all day, not socialize, not have a relationship with anyone, including yourself, and you will tuck that dog right next to you through it all. With pride in your voice, you say, "I adopted you. I rescued you. I will take care of you, and love you. But, I want you to want me all the time and stay with me. I won't change my lifestyle for you, but you didn't have any lifestyle (at least not a good one until I adopted you), so this is what you will be for me." Most human beings would have a hard time if that was imposed on them. It is unhealthy and toxic.

In the worst kind of situation, when we rescue an animal because we are alone, lonely, without love, wanting to give love to something or someone, and that part of our life is empty, we tend to give our attention and what we think is love to an animal who we rescue in order to fill the void and emptiness we have created in our lives. The dog then becomes the object of our affections, and therefore should suffer as we do. But in the long run, we are the only ones who can take ownership of our own neuroses, downfalls, and shortcomings. To fill the void based on this type of motivation and intent in order to avoid facing the responsibility of where we have put ourselves in life, and therefore not take ownership of our existence at that moment or how we got there, is the most selfish and self-serving reason to rescue and "take care of" a dog. This simply isn't fair.

Of course, I strongly encourage adoption, but we should only adopt animals from rescues for the right reasons—to take an animal out of a bad situation and let them have a life again, a life that allows the dog the ability to be a real dog, whether you live in the city or the country, it doesn't matter. Love the dog, let him be a best friend and companion, let him love you, and encourage growth. You smile when you see your dog being, simply, a dog. You support and encourage that as your dog supports you when you are in your natural light. As you would want your dog to grow and be happy, so should you.

Chapter Eight

Loss of Identity

As I considered what to include in this book, this was a very important chapter for me. I toyed with whether to address this topic or not because, when I have to confront it in a session, it tends to be a very touchy subject for everyone involved, including me. However, because it is common in so many animals, I decided it needed to be written.

One of the major characteristics that human beings and animals share, specifically dogs, is that of being solid in their identity. If we humans don't have a hold on our identity, then just about everything else fails. Our circumstances in life seem confusing and connections to our self and the outside world seem nearly impossible. We want to scream "who am I?" at the top of our lungs hoping to God that we get an answer or something that propels us forward into a clearer realm of understanding.

To illustrate the loss of ability to live out our true natures, I have a story about a little Chihuahua I recently met.

Sammy

She is a girl but was clearly given a boy's name. That's fine, but she also had a male companion who never had a dog before and really had wanted a big boy dog. Sammy was little, but tough. She wasn't allowed to socialize very often with any other dogs, and at home her human companion treated her in a rough and tumble way. All the while, he never truly identified that he ever really loved her. Sammy knew she was a girl, but she brushed her feminine nature aside so she could seem more male and so her human companion would love and acknowledge her. If he needed a boy dog to love, then that is what Sammy would be.

The problem was Sammy had gotten herself into a horrid mess. Her behavioral plan wasn't working, and when I was introduced to her, she was a sad and very confused little dog. She didn't know who or what she should be.

Any time Sammy had an opportunity to socialize with other dogs, the other dogs would give her a hard time. Before she would even get involved with them, Sammy would cry and scream and bark. She was basically saying, "I am confused. I am little. I am a girl but I am supposed to act like a tough boy dog. I never get let out to be a true dog. Frankly, I am a mess. Stay away from me, stay away from me. Where is my identity?"

This case involved a loss of identity for a dog and a severe loss of identity for the human companion as well. I found this out as revealed by the dog's energy when working with the family. The beauty about animals is that they are not selfish. When I am working with them, they not only let me know what is going on with them, but with everyone in the family. They ask, "How can we *all* be helped?"

It is never just the dog—it is always the family unit. This attitude is derived from that wonderful pack mentality that we as human beings don't always subscribe to.

As soon as I was ready to restore identity to this wonderful little animal, she effortlessly stepped into her natural light. No barking, no hesitancy, no chaos, and no disturbance. I offered it and Sammy gladly, quietly, and respectfully walked into it. At the same time, her human companion now felt safe to say he loved her for who she was and nothing more. He truly loved Sammy as a tough, beautiful little girl who deserved to go out and discover everything about her true dog self, and told Sammy he was ready to support and promote her socialization with other dogs. Sammy accepted what her human companion was now giving her, and it was done. You could see a light around Sammy that didn't exist before, and she was immediately living and functioning in the moment of her rediscovery. And, she loved every single second of it!

Sammy is an example of how animals can teach and guide us to our true identity. However, we must not forget that at the same time we also have the ability to take animals very far away from their own natural state and that the destruction of their identity can be worse than we ever imagined.

Because we possess that ability, this is a cautionary tale. We have become, as a society, too comfortable with the unfamiliar beings living inside our collective skin. We are lazy and fearful about wanting to know who we really are. We have extinguished some of the boundaries that set us apart as individuals. We have seen it in our own lives time and time again. If we can learn to control our energy for ourselves first and foremost, get acquainted with it, and know that its source lies within us, then the energy flowing out from each of us is cleaner and clearer, which, in turn, keeps everything cleaner and clearer for all of us.

Rediscovering your true nature, recognizing and knowing your true identity, and being in the moment, as animals are, help us learn how to deal with so many situations—how to love, enjoy, react, eat, socialize, and just be. Life is limitless. It is a concept I try to learn from daily. It's not always easy and that's why it is so wonderful if you happen to have a dog as a teacher. Learn from them. Learn how to love the process of exploration, the struggles that come with it, and be open to finding whatever knowledge it brings.

Since we are a society that has mastered the loss of identity, resolving an identity crisis is a very difficult process. We are all masters of disguise, putting on one mask after another until one day we throw one more mask on and realize we haven't taken the other ten off. Then we can't for the life of us find who the true individual really is.

In our desperate attempt to know who we are, we run into the closet, throw every mask we ever had into a pile, and shuffle through them all in the hope that one of the masks will make some sense. We long to recognize the raw face, the original soul, and the personality we know ourselves to be. Yet, sometimes the struggle is so intense we drop to our knees, look in the mirror, and have no idea who the hell we see reflected back. Our soul is gone, our heart is no longer connected and we wouldn't know our true self if it patted us on the back and said, "Hey, I am right here!"

Getting used to one's real identity is quite a wonderful and new adventure: the ground feels different and at times a bit shaky; smells are different, likes and dislikes change, and more. This is why I want people with whom I am working to walk in their new skin for a little bit before coming back to me to be cleared of all their stagnant energy and experience a full soul retrieval. In this way, although the process is still serious, it is much kinder.

As to how an identity crisis manifests in animals, I see all too often, whether meeting dogs on the street or working with them, that we humans have handed an identity to our dog that meets our own desires and state of mind. We do this by placing issues as well as stereotypes onto them to suit our needs, dimming their true light. In doing this, their dog nature can become lost. In contrast, there are plenty of dogs out there that are comfortable swimming in their true self and are lucky to have human companions who are also very content and happy in their own skin, allowing their animal to exist in its true nature, all the while appreciating and encouraging their unique identity. In these instances, both the animal and the human being are playing in their own zone and know exactly what and who they are.

It doesn't take much for dogs to recognize an identity crisis in another dog. When dogs run into another group of dogs or stop to sniff each other and say hello, they can tell right off the bat, even before making contact, if the other dogs are solid and comfortable or whether any of them don't have a grip on their own dog identity. How can we tell? Usually the behavior looks like this: the other dogs won't approach to sniff that dog and say hello, they aren't curious about the dog, they act out a bit, or they don't want anything to do with the dog. As human beings, we often socialize, function, and live without ever knowing our true identity, and virtually no one, I mean no one, will detect it. Interesting—this is not so in the canine world. It is almost entirely not tolerated.

Chapter Nine

Opening the Heart Center

About a year ago when I started writing, I was going on my second year of living without an animal. After the loss of my Bassett Hounds, Lucy and Lilly, I became completely indifferent to the idea of ever including another dog in my life. I convinced myself that since I worked with animals all the time and was such an advocate, that involvement could be enough. Throughout all my evenings spent sitting in solitude writing, I would sometimes wipe the tears from my face when I was done, shut down the computer, sit in the quiet, look around, and see exactly that . . . I was alone. The deaths of Lucy and Lilly were my final disconnect.

On a chilly fall evening in September two years ago, while wearing a full back brace, I lay on the cold tile floor of the veterinary hospital until 2:30 in the morning. Three days after my first back surgery, I received clearance from my surgeon that I was okay to move forward in my life. It was in that very moment that my beautiful dog Lilly decided it was safe for her to stop battling her terrible disease. I was locked into a moment where I felt my life was going to stop as soon as Lilly departed. It was a realization I never wanted to come to, about an event with which I would never need assistance. All I wanted was that when the time came, Lily would pass in the comfort of our home with me guiding the journey—safe, peaceful, and free.

That evening at the vet hospital, I was presented with a situation I hoped would never come. After trying to remove various amounts of fluid from Lilly's lungs, a process which continued into the wee hours of the morning, our mission was halted. It was past the point of turning this around. As the emergency vet explained what was happening, I already knew it was time to let go. The agony was overwhelming. In those moments, I lost faith, I lost hope, and I felt completely powerless. Looking up at the vet, I quietly declared, "I want to go with her. I am ready. I want to leave with Lilly. I don't want to be here anymore." Obviously, that was a reality this veterinarian was not going to step into. Yet, in my core, I felt that once Lilly left this Earth, I would be desolate. In that moment, I disconnected from my soul, my Heart Center, and everything in between.

As I started to move energy through Lilly, I saw her sister Lucy (who had passed a few months before) come sit next to me, along with six of Lilly's guides. All of them were huddled energetically around me like a warm blanket. "I am ready for her," Lucy spoke quietly to me. My hair was being stroked lightly by what I felt to be my lead Spirit Guide. My body grew cold, and I guided Lilly to run and chase the rabbits with her sister.

When Lucy passed those months before, we were home and needed no assistance. Lucy told me when the time was right, and I quickly sent energy through her to make it a very quick departure and an even quicker journey across. Through me, Lucy sailed away, and that beautiful personal moment I will hold with me always.

Both of their journeys sent a vibration out to me that, at the time, provided no idea of the changes they would bring. Lucy and Lilly guide me daily. The work needed for me to reconnect to my soul and Heart Center after such tragedies has been a boot camp that I put myself through and for which I am so thankful. Their guidance and support have propelled me into an even greater existence, and my gifts when dealing within the Metaphysical world have taken me into a realm I could have never imagined.

Just as I needed to work on opening my Heart Center, I have been called on numerous occasions to work with people to open their Heart Centers, whether to connect them to their animals or to themselves. It is not an easy task because we inevitably connect our Heart Center to our Mind Center (including our brain). We let the energetic capacity of the mind/brain control what our heart should feel, how it should respond, when we will open our hearts, and when we won't. It is not the easiest process to decipher. Is it your heart feeling the emotion, or is it your mind transferring what you think you should do with your heart? It's confusing, I know. When you hear people use the phrase, "Follow your heart, not your head," it can leave many saying to themselves, "How the hell should I exactly do that?" Much easier said than done! In order to better understand all this, let's first consider the basics, and answer some fundamental questions.

What is the Heart Center and what is its energy? Your Heart Center is focused completely in the present, and four of its characteristics are compassion, harmony, healing, and love. Its "senses" do not come from the physical but from feeling senses (not emotions, per se, but intuition and inner knowing). The Heart Center recognizes the truth of what exists in the moment, in the now. The energy emanating from the Heart Center because of its characteristics is therefore warm and revitalizing, and gives us the ability to express gratitude, peace, calm, balance, wholeness, and unity. The Chakra color associated with the Heart Center is green, symbolizing harmony, creativity, health, abundance, and nature. The Heart Center is the combination of Soul and Spirit.

What is the Mind Center and what is its energy? Your Mind Center (including your brain) understands information based on your five senses (visual, auditory, tactile, olfactory, and taste). Your brain cannot differentiate between your thoughts (what you "see" in your mind) and the sensory information sent to it. Through your Mind Center, you have the ability to reason and think, and be rational and detached. The Mind Center is all about the past and future, not what is in the present, but what was and what may be. The energy emanating from the Mind Center is cool, and the Chakra color most often associated with mental energy is yellow, symbolizing mental alertness, analytical thought, and thinking rather than feeling.

It is common knowledge that the brain has two hemispheres, and our learning skills and how we acquire knowledge usually have a preference depending upon which side of our brain is dominant, the left or the right.

The left side of the brain is the language center, and information courses through it in a logical and sequential manner. The right side is more visual, and information is processed intuitively and holistically. The left side perceives time in a linear way as either past or future, and rarely lives in the present. The right side is more open to thinking in the present, in the here and now. We, of course, develop both sides of our brains. We exchange and share information between the two hemispheres through a large bundle of nerve fibers that sends electromagnetic neuronal messages back and forth. This is how the brain communicates with itself and keeps connected.

If only we had such an obvious concrete connection mechanism between the Mind and the Heart!

Since we do not, how then do the Heart Center and Mind Center work together and stay connected? The Heart needs no reason to feel; it is intuitive and instinctive, whereas the Mind provides justifications for its thinking based on rational decisions that it makes over and over again until it is conditioned. The Mind becomes limited because of its conditioning and the disruptive energy caused by its ego-based decisions. When this happens and the Mind cannot come up with an answer to a problem or it cannot heal a wounded experience, it must move beyond the dilemma to resolve it and/or heal the wound. How does it do this? It reintegrates with its Heart Center. This desire to reintegrate requires a higher level of conscious awareness, which is our feeling, non-judgmental consciousness that lives within the Heart Center. The energies between the two Centers connect when the reintegration takes place, and the struggle ends. And in this way, the Mind follows the Heart, and not the other way around.

What causes the Heart and Mind Centers to disconnect? As mentioned earlier, the Heart Center holds the combination of Soul and Spirit. The Mind Center holds the ego and is based on thinking rather than feeling. The ego spends every waking conscious hour trying to avoid psychic and bodily pain, and trying to stay safe. It accomplishes this by retreating from the psyche and the body into its own mental domain until the Mind and Body disconnect. In the process, the Heart Center is forgotten and the Mind Center convinces itself it is the Soul Energy Center. The Heart's feelings and intuition become inaccessible, and the Mind moves further away from the Heart until the Mind Center and Heart Center disconnect. Much like the chapter called "Balancing Alpha Energy," the Mind Center becomes the "alpha" and the Heart Center the "submissive." When this occurs, the Mind takes the role of dictator, completely dominating the Heart, and everything is thrown out of balance. We begin to stumble over ourselves wondering why we can't fully feel the things we know innately that we should, until the Heart Center closes down.

It is usually never just one moment in time that alters the Heart Center. It could have been that the core of the problem was in development long ago, or that it was a particular horrid moment as a child that closed our hearts. Or, it may have been a life-altering event or tragedy that occurred later as an adult. It doesn't really matter when the final Heart Center connection was severed. What does matter is what caused the closure in order for us to heal the source wound, reawaken the Spirit, and reintegrate the Heart and Mind.

How exactly do we reopen the Heart Center and reconnect the Heart and Mind? It is always important to keep in mind that when reconnecting the Heart Center, the process is anything but speedy. It most likely will not happen on the first attempt, and maybe not even the next. But each time one attempts the reconnection, the energetic channel widens. The first step toward healing is to identify the source wound that closed the Heart Center. This usually requires raising our consciousness, our awareness, and our energy flow and vibration which can be accomplished in a variety of ways—meditation, centering and grounding, energy healing, and other forms of spiritual practice. Once identified, the next step is to take ownership of the wounded experience. That accomplished, the next step is to move it out energetically by reclaiming our higher feeling awareness centered in the Heart and use it to remove the thoughts that supported the negative conditioning. This shift creates the transformation that reconnects you energetically to your Heart Center, reopens your Heart, and returns you to a heart-based consciousness. Your soul, spirit, and intuitive feelings are reawakened. All that is left is to reconnect and reintegrate the Heart and Mind Centers.

Reintegration takes place when we reverse the previous disconnection process. That is, by using our higher feeling awareness with our reopened Heart Center, the Heart's feeling and intuition become accessible again, and the Heart Center reclaims its position as the primary energetic director, or the "alpha." The Mind Center once again returns to the "submissive" position, follows the Heart energetically, and moves back toward the Heart Center until they reconnect. Back in the Heart, beyond the fear and doubt of the Mind, we have regained our balance and are free to love and express gratitude and joy again.

When outlining the various chapters of this book, I had a specific direction regarding whose story I would use as the example for each central theme. In this chapter on opening the Heart Center, I had the clear intention to use myself.

Emma

After a long winter spent in New York, I decided to return to Los Angeles and make a bright, warmer climate my home base. I am from New York and certainly thrive there, but I felt traveling to and from the East Coast was a better solution than living there full time.

On one warm summer day in Los Angeles, I had some time between clients. As I drove to satisfy my craving for a sandwich, I found myself steering in a very different direction. A few of my favorite haunts rolled by, but I continued driving. I wondered to myself, "Where am I going exactly?" With only a couple of hours to spare, I knew this mini-adventure needed to work itself out fairly quickly. As I entered the city of Burbank, winding around a few corners, it struck me that I could be driving toward the Burbank Pound. Being led by a whole different force, I was still a bit reluctant to continue on this impromptu journey. "Why am I going to the Pound?" I declared. "I can't get a dog. I am not ready yet. Plus, I have to travel often, and it's just not the right time to do this. I need to turn around!"

Meanwhile, through the entirety of this rationalizing conversation with myself, I was still driving to the damn

Pound! Turning into the parking lot, I shut off the car and said out loud, "Okay, we are only looking today. I will honor this journey, but I am serious—this is just a diversion."

I got out of the car and slowly walked toward the facility. As I opened the front door, a flood of desolate energy overcame me. So many lost souls wastefully thrown aside, hoping for the chance to expand their lives. Walking through a shelter, a pound, or a rescue is a difficult experience for every one of us. Yet for me, I must shut down so much of what I hear energetically from the animals because the conversations overwhelm me. Sometimes what I hear and what I need to communicate back can get so overpowering that I have to purposely shut off all energetic communication unless it is to instill a sense of calm or a feeling of security. I want the animals to know I understand, and to allow me, even for a moment, to ease any of their worry and confusion.

What I ultimately do when I am in that environment is to send great forces of healing energy to all the animals with whom I come in contact. Then, I surge the healing energy through the whole facility in hopes of reaching each and every animal that is housed there. After that, I must be aware of what I will allow in and what I will expose myself to. So often, the most I can do is to help clear and ease their minds while they are there. It certainly is not an easy thing for them to experience, and I would love to empty the Pound of every animal present and take them somewhere beautiful and freeing to live. It is heartbreaking to say the least . . . very heartbreaking.

As I walked down the long hallway of indoor/outdoor cages, I moved as if I were being directly led to a specific dog. While I continued on, I hadn't stumbled onto one until I came upon a cage with the sign "poodle mix." Inside was a small dog, quite shaggy, whose face I could barely see through all the long ringlets. As I crouched down in front of the cage, I saw this little animal start to walk up to the front of her kennel. She was in a low submissive walk, practically slithering in fear as she approached. "Hey," I said energetically, "don't give me that submissive stuff. Let that go if you're going to walk up to me. Just walk. There is nothing to fear. Let that go now!"

Her eyes looked straight through me. She wasn't energetically communicating to me yet, which made me wonder. It was, however, very clear that this dog had a serious intention, was very much aware of who I was, why I came, and most importantly, she definitely knew I was coming today. She had been briefed, so to speak. But, she was going to keep her mouth shut until she was 100% certain. Quite frankly, I found this very endearing as it is something I apply to my own life. "Okay," I thought, "now this is getting interesting!"

I could tell she understood what I said about her crawling submissively because after a while she changed her whole approach. Her head raised, her shoulders became broader, her eyes widened, and she took a full upright stance on all fours. With a deep breath, she walked to the front of her cage and presented herself to me.

The first thing I noticed was that her eyes were so rich with wisdom for such a young dog. The Pound listed her age as two years, but I felt she was no more than one-and-a-half. Again, although she hadn't said a word to me energetically, not one word, she was definitely listening. This animal was well aware of everything I am, what I do, how I do it, and every detail of my personal history. I suddenly realized I was trying a little extra hard to appear somewhat "cool" or "unique," as if to impress this little dog in some way. I don't believe I have ever done that before with an animal. If the truth be told, I was falling very short in my performance. And she was not amused!

I couldn't help but be curious about this little dog, and clearly needed to look into her a bit further. As I searched for someone to help me, I located an attendant who was working the cages. "I would like to see the little poodle mix in Cage 3," I said. "She doesn't have much paperwork, and it looks like she is scheduled to be put down in a few days."

The attendant said, "Yes, she came in a couple of days ago and is on an extra day hold in case someone wants to claim her. So, we can't do any visits until her hold time is up." As I listened to him describe this dog, it was as if she was just the number on her cage. Everything about it was business and routine. Although he seemed like a nice individual, he was completely desensitized and disconnected, and looked at these dogs like they were Sony televisions at Best Buy! Move them in, move them out, and nothing in between.

I walked to the front desk to get some more specific information. "Hi, I was interested in the little female poodle."

The woman sitting behind the desk looked up and said, "They are identified according to cage numbers and nothing else. We don't know what dogs we have here if we don't have a number code." After I gave her the information she needed, the woman told me that on Wednesday (two days from the day I visited), I needed to call in the morning and see if she had been claimed. After that, if more than one person wanted her, they would have a lottery. The person whose name was drawn would get her.

"Hmm, that sounds a little strange," I said. "Isn't this about finding the best home for the dog? Is there no interview process or even a consideration that whoever draws the lottery ticket could be an asshole?"

This woman looked up at me and gave me a look that almost shot me right out the front door! "That's the way we do it," she pronounced. "We don't worry about who takes the dog just as long as someone takes it. Now, if you want to give this a shot, then call on Wednesday morning and we'll take it from there."

I stood there for a moment and thought, "Well, as the Universe is leading me, and if it is meant to be, when I make the call on Wednesday morning and am supposed to have her, then I know this was exactly what I was scared to acknowledge on my drive over . . . Destiny."

Wednesday morning arrived and as I sipped my morning coffee, I dialed the number I was given. "Hi, my name is Jocelyn Kessler. I was in on Monday looking at a poodle mix in Cage Number Three. I just wanted to see if anyone had claimed her, or if I need to be part of a lottery"

"Well, Miss Kessler," the receptionist responded, "it looks like no one has claimed her, and nobody wanted to put their name in the lottery for her either. So, if you want to meet her and take it further, I would come down and do so now."

My breath got deeper and I felt a surge of energy to my Heart Center that made me very uncomfortable. The energy was nervous, erratic, and completely bewildering to me. What was I thinking? There was an awkward silence from me on the phone, and then the voice on the other end said, "Hello! What do you want to do?" After taking a long, very fulfilling breath, I said, "I will see you in an hour. Please don't let anyone else touch her until I get there."

At that moment of decision, I walked into a transitional energy I knew I had been avoiding, and couldn't any longer. It was in that instant that my life drastically changed, and I wasn't at all sure if I was ready for the journey I was about to begin. What I did know was that the energy directing me was so strong and so innate that I had to listen.

So, I put coffee in the to-go mug and me in the driver's seat, and I was off. I drove in silence as I made my way again through Burbank en route to the Pound. What normally is a lot of stop and go traffic was clear sailing this morning. The streetlights seemed perfectly timed, and everyone in front of and behind me moved without interference.

My promise to myself when I arrived was to remain neutral because I had not yet formed an opinion about this whole new situation. It is important, as I so often express to my clients, to not let your energy become erratic or allow your mind to take over. If the mind overpowers the heart energy, it can lead to the creation of thoughts that are non-existent realities, and can bring the individual out of the proper electromagnetic field the Universe is so desperately trying to keep you in. In this case, the individual I am talking about was me!

I struggle with the same issues we all do. I have just kept myself aware enough to know when I am slipping out of what appears to be the natural order of things. That is when I take a deep breath and ask to be grounded and balanced, and then the rest comes as it should. It is very difficult to do this as it is happening. Keeping yourself aligned when you are at a weak point is when it most matters, for me or for anyone.

Up until this point in my life, I had worked for a long time on many of my core issues, such as harboring a destructive path, and had cleared the main sources of those types of energetic disruptions. That is, except for the pesky little core issue regarding my inability to trust my vulnerability, which emanates from the Heart Center. I have struggled with that but have finally learned to trust that my heart is stronger than I truly know.

All the work I do on myself, as well as with others, has kept my Soul, Mind, and Heart connected. Being energetically connected to myself and the Universe has made life so brilliant. I am surprised and appreciative every moment of every day, without a doubt. Yet, to be honest, staying neutral and not feeding at the same time on my inability to trust my vulnerability was a trouble spot I needed to transform in order to move into the next level of conscious awareness. I had to make myself cognizant of going with the moment and only with the moment, much like the little animal I was en route to visit.

She, like all animals, was in the moment. She didn't judge her situation or me or what would possibly occur. She knew just what she needed to know now. It is an insanely smart approach and something animals have innately. If we can embrace and adopt this part of their nature, it could possibly be one of the biggest cognitive breakthroughs for human beings, affecting not only how we direct our energy but how we conduct our lives. It's extraordinary because it is clean and allows us to act upon pure instinct and intuition, and nothing else. It certainly makes for a more pleasurable life. That is something I can state with complete and honest certainty!

If ever I was obligated to practice what I so often preach it was at that decision-making moment in which I found myself. My drive in the car was effortless, and my mind and body were a clean slate, ready to act as I needed to and feel as I needed to, without churning up disruptive energies from the past that were now non-existent.

Walking into the Pound, I sauntered up to the front desk and asked to meet "Cage 3, please."

They told me to "Walk to the last waiting room at the end of the hallway and we will bring her in. She is getting groomed now so they will just finish that up and then you two can meet." I took my orders and sat quietly in the little visiting room.

Fifteen minutes or so passed and I thought, "Are they picking her up from the day spa or what?" The door slowly opened and a young man walked in with her. She was newly coiffed and smelled like citrus. Her little head still needed some blow drying, but I finally could see her eyes and her shape. I felt her energy immediately—she was completely and utterly neutral! She was in the zone.

As she hung in the arms of the attendant, we watched one another.

"Would you like to hold her?" he said. She and I both knew this was it. In less than ten seconds we would energetically connect. The vibrations between us grew stronger. As I reached out to her, I grabbed her under the shoulders. I didn't bring her into me right away.

"I want to see her face and eyes first," I said "before I do much more." The young man just smiled. He seemed more like a wallflower, almost inanimate, amid the tension stirring in the tiny little visitor room.

Dangling in front me, in what appeared to be a semi-catatonic state, this little dog just stared at me, almost ignoring me. I looked into her eyes and surged a vast amount of energy into her. This energy surge was not my usual approach with most animals. But in this case, she was clearly destined to be a very new, very out-of-the-blue addition to my life. I traveled through her energetically, and saw her history, past lives, and what she carried with her. If I was certain of anything in this moment it was that she never faltered, never blinked, *and* that she was surging the same energy right back at me!

I had yet to energetically utter one word to her, or her to me. What she was doing with my energy was very different . . . *very* different! She was outrageously connected metaphysically. I could see her whole existence in this moment, past moments, karmic moments, as well as her core issues. And at the same time, she so effortlessly saw all of mine.

I opened my mouth for the first time in several minutes. As I stared at her, I said, "You know, I don't normally do poodles, not exactly my cup of tea, at least for my personality."

She looked at me, never wavering, and I heard her energetic voice for the first time. "Well, I don't know if I like you so much," she said, "but I do know who you are, what you are about, and what you can do. And, it doesn't scare or intimidate me. This moment is by arrangement, and that's all you need to know. Now, let me get finished being groomed, go pay the hundred dollars to get me out of this place, and let's move on!"

I smiled and turned to the very patient handler and said, "I'll take her!"

One thing that I knew from the start was that I needed to save her and get her out of that place, no matter what. Whether she was for me, or for me to foster her and then give her to a wonderful home was yet to be determined. To be perfectly honest, that pesky core issue I spoke of earlier that I had done so much work on and thought I had cleared . . . well, it began to creep in again and we were having a "red alert" so to speak. This dog had identified my issue the first moment she laid eyes on me. One of the amazing things about her was that she already knew she wasn't in for the easiest ride. She knew she was home though, no matter what was going on in me, and she let me know she was here to change that. She knew she was never meant for anyone else. And she was right!

Let me introduce the dog that went by "she" and "little dog" for so long . . . that little dog is now named Emma. Welcome home!

Within the first week I had Emma, it became very evident to me that she travels on a frequency I have only seen in dogs a few times in my life. She sees into a higher realm and is Spirit sensitive. In fact, she interacts with Spirits on a daily basis—they are part of her everyday existence just as normal worldly tangible interactions are. It's really quite remarkable to watch.

Also during that first week, I cried nightly. I am someone who is not a crier, not because I pride myself in it, but rather because I tend to stay more disengaged until it's absolutely necessary for me to go there. And when it is necessary, I own every minute of it! I will use a good cry, with all its intensity, for regenerative purposes whenever possible. Yet once the purge is done, I am good to go. I clear myself fully, do various energetic restoration meditations, and know that the purge was worth every second.

With respect to Emma, I had to come to terms with the obvious guilt I had from the loss of my dog Lilly and how she passed. My guilt was not fully cleared. There still was a bit of dark neurosis inside of me connected to my feelings about Lilly and to anything that would allow my Heart to really breathe again.

Although I was Soul connected, and my Heart Center was connected to my Crown Chakra, it was as if I had a "faulty wire" connecting my heart to my head. Whenever I did my own personal work, occasionally a little spark would fly between the two. Unconsciously, I knew that wasn't enough. Yet for days, I made every excuse to not fix the problem. After a week of gut wrenching sobbing, I decided to step up and take the necessary action to find the solution. I knew it was time to truly open my Heart Center again and vibrate out a much different frequency. So instead of calling an electrician, I just looked down at Emma!

A few weeks passed, and all we really did was look at one another in our own separate space. Now many would say, "That's ridiculous, weren't you just consumed by her and she by you?" Well, no one has ever accused me of not having an interesting approach. I believe very strongly in learning to appreciate one's space no matter whether you are a dog, cat, human, horse, etc. We have lost that concept. In this case, I was lucky to find a dog that very much valued the space she needed for herself and understood it was very much the same for me.

Emma had been kicked around a bit before me. We all understand that being kicked around can cause years of damage. For Emma, this new direction her life had taken with me would determine if she was ready to move into the next phase of her life. And interestingly enough, it proved to be the same for me. We were mirror images of each other. I saw Emma longing for confidence to trust and really love again. This was going to require being patient not only with me, but with herself. This time around, we were both going to learn to open and love again.

Seemingly a little rough around the edges lately, I looked to Emma to soften me when I got too strong. She was in a vulnerable stage and was quick to appreciate my strength. Yet at the same time, Emma was constantly looking to me to release some of my strength to her. In addition, she was even quicker to ask me to be more playful.

Emma became a wonderful teacher and student almost instantly. As I showed her that she was safe and her life had begun again, I saw marked improvement in her daily. Normally when I would approach her for any reason, Emma would drop down into the submissive position on her back and then start crawling along the floor. She was programmed by a human being to not trust any kind of interaction. Adding insult to injury, she also had a marked fear of being hit. This was our biggest obstacle and one that needed to be rectified for Emma's sake. I wanted to get her past that conditioned level so she could move into a brighter, more trusting, state of mind. As I watched her, it became even more apparent to me how similar we were. I was also very reluctant to get involved with much human interaction. I guess you could say I was going into a submissive state as well whenever I would meet someone new. My wall went up right away.

My approach to create a safe environment for Emma was to always stay neutral when touching her. When I first arrived home, I wouldn't touch her right away. We had small conversations, but I didn't go straight for her to pick her up and overwhelm her. After a few minutes, I would quietly sit next to her and she would wander up slowly to me to find her comfort. Eventually, that fear of interaction didn't hold the same energy for Emma when I came home to greet her. Instead, she would throw a ball my way when I walked in the door and that was her way of saying, "Let's have interaction but in a playful way."

Emma loves squeaky toys. My other dogs didn't care about toys very much, yet Emma simply adores them! I used that love of toys as a healing technique to get her out of fear, which also enabled me to soften instantly and just play a bit with her. Not only did this transform me, but Emma made marked improvement in her confidence through play. It was quite an interesting concept. I had no understanding or knowledge of that healing technique until Emma.

If we were outside throwing a ball and someone would come up to pet Emma or say hello to me, Emma wouldn't let them come right up to her. Instead, she would drop her toy in front of them as if to say, "I am branching out, but I am doing it safely by sharing my toy and my space without overwhelming myself. I will include you, but let's play together first." A brilliant concept she had put into place—holding boundary and space while seeing what the other animal or the person was made of. Clearly I had instigated this play concept for Emma, but she took it, ran with it, and made it her own!

Emma's energy was getting stronger daily. She was opening her Heart Center and letting go of her old ways of interacting. She showed herself, as well as me, that we can all take a little time to get to know each other, and no particular way is better than another. The lesson was, "I will include you a bit, and see what you are made of, and then I can start building some trust."

Emma started to become, for herself and for me, the epitome of conducting oneself within a kind and appropriate space. We all give up too much personal space too soon. This is not to say that hiding or fear is the answer. But, being open, neutral, and in the moment gives us the time to build respect, trust, and a happier Heart Center. This proved to be both Emma's and my greatest asset. And, Emma was using this technique with flying colors! She was smiling and enjoying life more and branching out, and I started to see how much fun she really was.

Emma came into my life when I was working with many new ways and theories concerning the use of energetic vibration and restoring balance through animals. Yet, I didn't actually do any hands-on energetic work with Emma right away because I wanted us to first get accustomed to each other. I knew she was definitely not ready for it and neither was I. We needed to first establish our boundaries, and once established, it would just happen . . . and it did.

After a very long day, I came home to a little dog sitting at the foot of my bed just staring at me. She didn't walk over to see me, or get overly excited upon my arrival. In fact, it was quite the opposite!

"What do you have going on up there, Emma?" I said. Her eyes were very serious. After all the days I had needed to work on abandoning Emma's submissiveness when I walked through the door, tonight a shift had taken place. After one month of finding our "space," it was time for us to work on Heart Center.

I stared at her as she sat in this very regal position, and I said, "I don't know if I am ready to heal like this, Emma. If I connect like that, it will change everything." Slowly, Emma got off the bed and onto the rug, quietly lying on her side with one eye looking up at me. She was neutral in energy and in full release. She was ready to work with me. As I sat down near her, I closed my eyes and started to ask for my Animal and Human Guides. The room started to fill quickly. So much so that it was getting really crowded. I asked for some room.

I then asked for Emma's guides to come in as well. Surprisingly enough, I discovered that some of her guides are children. It was very beautiful to see as they made their way into the room. They were playful, loving, and so very warm. When I say "they" made their way into the room, I am describing an energetic presence. In this case, not only could I see and hear them clearly, but I could also smell, taste, and feel every single energetic presence in that room. It was phenomenal!

Emma's tail started to wag as I set my right hand on her Heart Center, and my left hand on my Heart Center. The right side represents the masculine, and the right hand gives or transmits energy; the left side represents the feminine, and the left hand receives energy. It has always been my right side that has dominated most of my personal existence. I continued for many years to feed that right-side-dominant energy like we were eating at an all-you-can-eat buffet . . . daily! I had once needed to build up my masculine energy, but I had given it so much strength that I sealed up my Heart Center, and put the burden on my left or feminine side. I was battering myself for far too long. In that moment when I started to feel energy flow through my right hand into Emma's heart, I started to cry. Her heart was so alive and strong. Once I started to energetically travel through the white light washing over me, for the first time I saw Emma's true abilities. She was able to travel in the energy I do, and interact with the spirit world right alongside me! She knew all her guides and, in fact, she knew mine too.

All of a sudden I felt a hand on my shoulder. It was the energy of a child about age five or so, female. "What happened to your inner child, Jocelyn?" the young voice said. I felt the room become very cold, which is not always the case for me. I can feel spirit presence without change of temperature, yet at times when the message or the energetic frequency is really high, I can sense change of temperature as well. Emma took very slow, big breaths. I knew this dog was special, but until that evening, I had no idea how special her gifts were. As I felt blood flow through my heart as if I had taken my first breath, I knew that Emma wouldn't let me down nor would I her.

Before removing my hands from an animal or human, I always protect and seal the energetic space I worked in. Yet, as I prepared to remove my hand from Emma and ask for protection, something told me to open my eyes. I looked down and Emma was just staring at me. Her energy said, "You don't need the whole song and dance tonight, let's just go do something different now!"

We jumped up and decided to go on a beautiful evening walk. As I put Emma's harness on, for the first time since I got her, she didn't bow her head in conditioned fear while I put the harness over her head. Instead, she stood regally, head raised with a newfound dignity as I hooked her in. At the same time, I experienced an electrical current of energy that flowed through me and allowed me to breathe a little easier. As we set off down the street, the night sky took on a whole new meaning for us. My senses were heightened. I thought I was the only one affected in that way, but when I looked down at Emma, I acquired a whole new respect for her. For the first time as she walked down the dark streets she had once feared so much and with seemingly a very weak sense of smell, she was now picking up scents that made her prance with excitement. Our Universe felt different to us. As we aimlessly walked for about an hour, we did so both happily and contented with the significant transition we were brave enough to walk through *together*.

From that day on I kept myself quite aware of my own energy so that I wouldn't allow into my mind anything that could change the balanced energy that had been created. It was hard not to be aware. I felt ashamed of myself that as I had showed others how to open their Heart Center, mine had been closed. I had no idea it took this little "Cage No. 3" to shed the vast amount of light needed to heal us both. Emma is my mirror image and teacher. When my energy shifts into an unnatural or conditioned state, she picks that up and reacts usually in exactly the same unnatural way, and it forces me to stop and check my awareness. I know she is right every single time. Absolutely!

Since opening our hearts energetically, the changes within both of us were very beautiful, especially in Emma. We have both received such significant gifts. Neither of us could keep up with the changes occurring at such amazing speed. Emma started to become much freer with allowing her more playful self out. She gave herself quality time to really enjoy herself when I would write.

As for me, my writing became much stronger, and my newly reconnected Heart Center allowed me to write more freely with a sense of vulnerability that I previously didn't know how to translate. Emma taught and showed me that being vulnerable, compassionate, and honest is something that can be done freely in the moment without any reservations. It is such a beautiful feeling that one would think it is easy to obtain, yet it is not.

As I encourage Emma to be confident to trust me and to trust where she is now, not where she was, Emma in turn has made me shockingly aware that I had fallen out of my moment. One day I found myself looking in the mirror to narrow in on a flaw (not exactly the best medicine; but no matter what I believe in, as I am a woman, I can have my moments too). Trotting in with one of her many squeaky toys, Emma dropped a rubber ladybug at my feet.

"Give me a second, Emma," I said as I started revving up to quietly attack myself in a weak moment. As Emma started to lightly kick me with her foot, I insisted, "Please, Emma, give me a second!" All of a sudden I heard this high-pitched bark, which is not one of Emma's usual vocal manipulations. "*Please, Emma!*" I pleaded. Then I decided to really hear her, tuned into the energy we had both created, and listened.

I bent down, picked her up, and all I heard energetically was, "I love you." That was all she said. It happened to be the first time I felt that from her and truly the first time I hugged her tight and without hesitation said, "I love you too!" The senseless process of personal degrading behavior that I had engaged in seemed almost trivial, and could only have occurred as a result of the Heart Center being disconnected.

Emma is not only my dog; she is also my friend, my ally, and my partner as we move together into the next learning transition of our lives. She certainly has kept up her end of the bargain by staying connected herself while keeping my energy in check. My gratitude is an understatement.

Emma and I moved into a new home not too long after our Heart Center session. As I gazed over to Emma (who was laughing and enjoying her bone without a care in the world), I could clearly see she was no longer cautious or fearful to reveal herself, and no longer afraid to show me how much she loves to be quirky. In turn, her playful, open, energetic vibration allowed me to learn to enjoy my time and my space in our new home and really "live" in my personal surroundings. I learned to enjoy the free moments as well as the occupied ones.

Perhaps one of the most interesting changes in Emma was her awareness of the spirit world. A couple of months after moving into our new house, I went to run a bath. I love taking baths, and I will take one at any time of the day or night—this one was about to occur roughly at midnight. On that particular evening, we had the music on in the house, and I had been dancing with Emma and throwing her toy (Emma is a big music lover, as am I).

When I proceeded to the tub, I noticed that Emma had taken over her own playtime and allowed me to have a nice bath. Leaving the door open so she could run in and out, I was able to lie in the tub and see her occupying her time. As my eyes closed and I sank into the warm water, I let my mind travel and found I was in deep relaxation. That was until I heard some kind of commotion. It seemed odd. My eyes slowly opened and without making any noise I quietly sat up a bit and looked out to where Emma was. I saw her running around the room chasing her toy and throwing it for herself while letting out these playful little barks. This was a very different side of Emma that I had never seen before, and I wanted to quietly observe.

As I peered out the door, I saw her in my hallway looking up at the ceiling and moving her head as if she was watching some kind of movement. She then wagged her tail, jumped up and down, and tossed the ball to something she was looking at in the corner. Then as she gently nudged it over, she waited for it to be thrown—very much like she does when she plays ball with me or with anyone else for that matter. At this point, I turned my head back to the bath, and before I knew it, I heard what sounded like the toy being thrown. When I looked up again, Emma was running across the room to retrieve the toy. Then she looked up toward the ceiling again and started to move along the hallway wall, letting out these little barks while intently watching movement above and around her.

When I got myself focused, I could sense that she was playing with what looked and felt like a spirit that seemed to be a mixed species breed of animal. It appeared to be something like a cross between a monkey and a cat. I know this sounds strange, but in the spirit world, animals have the ability to morph into what I call spiritual "hybrid" animals. This was one of those hybrids.

The first thing I do when I feel a presence in my home is to determine right away if it is traveling in dark or light energy, and if there is any harm present. In this particular case it was all good. The spirit and Emma were both very kind to each other. This play session lasted for about twenty minutes. She was enjoying this spirit to the fullest and vice versa. I was stunned because, although I knew there was some spirit activity in my home, I didn't know how much of it Emma could sense. Sensitive animals can be incredible when picking up or identifying spirits with whom they come in contact. Yet the surprise of the evening was how innate and practically organic Emma's interaction was for her. She was so effortless, and took the opportunity right in the moment. It was meant to be.

For a very long time, I had a huge struggle with the gift given to me to see, hear, and work with the spirit world while at the same time living in this world. It is not always easy. In fact, it has been my biggest struggle. I never declared myself the most normal individual in the world to begin with, and lord knows I have been called various names. That doesn't bother me as much as my personal struggle to live and love fully in this reality, while at the same time finding my place within the higher energy frequency that occupies the spirit world. I am in constant contact with both worlds—all day and every day. To be honest, it has caused me great distress at times. I repeatedly ask myself how to function fluidly in both.

Observing Emma interacting in the spirit world and our world was such a learning experience for me, and one that could only have happened after our opening the Heart Center session. Emma felt free and comfortable to live and play within the spirit world while being in this world, and never once acted as if there was any division. Nothing was confusing for her. Because of the trust Emma found within herself and in me, this made her interaction just as freeing for her as playing ball with me.

Since opening up to my Heart and Mind Center connection, I now know Emma was brought to me to understand that in the next chapter of my life I cannot possibly obtain the blessings coming to me without a Heart Center that is ready to be revealed and connected. When I say this, I mean that if our hearts do not radiate an energetic vibration that indicates we are open to the life force of everything that is love, we can eventually become energetically stagnant. That is what happened to me. Although I was trying to manage all my energy efficiently, I blatantly ignored a very fundamental connection.

From the day I drove to look for a dog, I was very much aware that I was being led to this little animal by the Universe and by my Guides. Fate stepped in and ushered a dog to me that was going to teach and remind me that without a Heart that could run at its greatest potential, I am nothing. I honor this blessing.

Almost daily, Emma and I sit in quiet and go into connection. It is part of my day whether I feel like it or not. We have gotten into a groove, so to speak. When I am slipping, she has no hesitation to energetically let me know that. In a very kind manner, she will pull me back to center. Not only do I now ask for it, I demand it!

The feeling of reconnection is sublime. There are always hardships. That's life. Yet, what already felt to me like an existence of sheer beauty and light, even through hard times, now has become a whole new open road, one that I had a hard time even finding directions to! Emma came to me because her Heart, although damaged, was the one bright star that could release me to know again what love is.

Chapter Ten

It's a Wrap

Together we have taken a journey through these pages. I commend and thank you for your sincere willingness to do so. By giving yourself such a road to travel, the biggest and most important step has been taken. Trust that the commitment to be open to the process of connection and soul retrieval has already allowed you to see yourself in a whole new light. Congratulations!

The catalyst for me to write this book has always been my belief in connection—connection to your animal and to yourself. We want and need connection yet we struggle to find it because our societal path has become so disorienting that we have taken ourselves off course. Connection in society is the compass that brings us back to clarity and balance, and promotes the even flow of universal energy. A collective harmony results that is in accord with our more tranquil minds and our clearer sense of direction. This harmony, of course, starts with you.

I hope this journey has brought you to the realization that it is okay to know and love who you are, to become more aware of how you feel, to form a friendship with your true self, and then, like Walt Whitman, to sing in full voice the Song of Yourself. Your internal harmony comes from the recognition and ownership of the mirror that reflects you in both your natural and unnatural light. The dissonance heard is when we make the conditioned choice to drape the mirror. This discordant act is what stops our life's progress. However, we know that we are ready to come out of hiding and do the hard work when we choose to rid ourselves of all our masks, cleanly connect with our genuine original self, and live our lives more freely and openly in both shadow and light. This freedom allows us to be more conscious of not only how we treat ourselves, but our treatment of others and our environment. Ultimately it dictates how, what, and to whom we give, and what we are destined to receive.

Energy works in quite an uncomplicated way. Once we connect to ourselves, we can then venture out and connect to another individual and then to another and another. This changes the vibrational energy and flow between each one of us and affects everyone with whom we come in contact. It actually switches all our energies.

I hope the Steps to Connect provided in Chapter Eleven will facilitate and encourage you to do energy work within yourself and with your dog. That energy, whether or not clear in the beginning, affects everyone we encounter. Period. It is a natural law—balanced, connected energy produces more of the same. Learning from animals how to live in the moment inspires contentment, and breeds a positive outlook that we all long to achieve. The practice of conscious awareness is a very powerful thing. It can improve your life and the lives of others.

When I considered how to wrap this up, I decided we could use a moment to take a breath and just be proud of the sheer beauty our dogs radiate. So, I thought it would be nice to share some of the wonderful things dogs encompass by giving you a few delightful traits of two more dogs I had the good fortune to meet while working with clients. As important as it is to make connections and do all the hard work, it is just as important for us to observe, celebrate and take pleasure in the shining light within which our dogs live.

Glory

When working with a little dog named Glory, the main theme for her and her human companion Jessica was balance. Both Glory and Jessica were searching for a more balanced life. Both enjoyed the "sweetness" of life yet felt some things were missing. As we worked to address the issues they shared, I came across a very interesting yet prudent trait that Glory possessed. It was a characteristic that probably traveled with her for lifetimes. And, Glory was terribly insistent to talk about it. It was her sheer love and need for *candy*!

Candy, in the form of just about every hard candy one could dream of. She loved it, craved it, and as a result her teeth weren't so great.

"If I could have candy with every meal—maybe a peppermint stick for breakfast, followed by a root beer barrel for a snack, and some cherry Life Savers for dinner—I would be perfectly content."

I started to laugh when I got this and said to Jessica, "Boy, she really loves candy. She can't stress that enough!"

Jessica in turn broke into laughter and in full force said, "Yes, yes, yes! That is so true. She steals candy. She looks for candy and devours it when she gets hold of it. I don't know where that comes from."

I then told Jessica that Glory also seemed to have quite an affinity for ice cream. "In fact, she could use a scoop as we speak."

Jessica was beside herself giggling. I relished in watching how beautiful her enjoyment was. "Every time I walk Glory and we pass by this wonderful ice cream shop, she stops at their front door and will not budge! She stares inside in complete amazement like a child. Then I usually go on in, get a small scoop of vanilla, and we share it. She has this look of heaven on her face."

As Jessica and I were talking, Glory lit up, indicating that this was definitely her element. Mind you, I am not suggesting that if your dog loves candy you should feed candy to them all day long! By all means, that is not what I am saying. It was just such an urgent and delightful topic for Glory to bring up. It was so childlike and clean. When Glory spoke of her love of candy, and then Jessica and I added so much energy and excitement of our own, it was as if Glory was floating on an energy stream of gum drops and lollipops. We took the ride with her. Through me, Glory could truly enjoy and play with her love of candy.

As the candy conversation continued, Glory ran around and looked at Jessica with a gleam in her eye. Then all of a sudden Glory sat right in front me and expressed a desire. So often dogs will focus on the serious, immediate, and necessary issues in the household, and then by energetically communicating to me, they make a point to let me know about something that is lighter or something that they love, miss, or want.

For instance, at the beginning of the session, almost all dogs immediately let me know about the serious concerns they have for their human companions, we do the work in session, and then the dog again energetically communicates to me they would like a special toy or some kind of treat for communicating their companions' needs. I also think it's so lovely and special when they do this because it's their way of giving themselves a reward for all their hard work. In Glory's case, she rewarded herself for being very present, in the moment, open to the connection to Jessica, and for working on all the serious things that needed to be addressed. In life, it is quite a beautiful and connected way to live, and essentially how we should all live! It promotes balance.

We needed to find a way Glory could balance her desire for all things sweet. She was willing to try but certainly did not want to give it up entirely. As Glory got very serious with me, she let me know that she really wanted a candy cane. Now, granted, it was around Christmas time. She was compelled to let me know she longed for a particular kind of candy cane; not a small one, but a regular full-sized candy cane! I giggled when I received that information, and asked Jessica, "Do you have candy canes in the house?" Jessica shook her head "no" and asked why.

"Well, Glory wants one and tends to like them this time of year. I am not saying to let her eat the whole candy cane, but the pure satisfaction of being handed one would be just glorious for her. That's what she wants."

Jessica laughed and we both found joy in such a very simple yet beautiful request.

Dogs have those wonderfully interesting little passions carried with them from their beginnings or sometimes picked up from their human companion. It was interesting that the real reason for Glory's presence in Jessica's life was to find balance, and as light and entertaining as the subject of candy was, clearly Glory's boundaries and balance with candy were almost nonexistent.

As much as I promote very clean eating for animals, I strongly felt a little candy in moderation was something Glory could have. It actually would go hand in hand with the serious work we did earlier in the session. Once we attain balance and then have our candy "fixes," whatever innocent amusement we celebrate will be appreciated even more as it makes life's little rewards so much more enjoyable. I guess you could say balance leads to a sweeter life.

That was the beauty about Glory and Jessica. They were both so childlike and free. If they could both work together to find balance, then when those innocent moments occurred, it would be even sweeter for them. That is why, in this case, when Jessica said perhaps she should never give Glory anymore candy, I disagreed. Now I am sure I will get a lot of heat for this, but quite frankly I stand by my theory. I thought candy could remain in Glory's life because I was confident in knowing Jessica would be able to assist Glory with that balance and obviously not feed her candy all the time. Glory could have those loving moments as long as the candy treats were used sparingly.

Whenever I leave a new client, I always write an email summary with some points to remember from our visit so the work stays in focus and we all stay connected. I never leave a client without some follow up. I am an advocate for "connection." Some of the work we do can be so intense that it is very important to make sure both the dogs and the human companions know they are truly special to me, and that I am aware and in their lives. This occurs as soon as I walk through the door. Support is so important and vital, and something I handle with care for every single session. After emailing Jessica, I received a lovely follow up from her thanking me for our time together, along with a little story. When reading it, I smiled because I could feel Jessica's energy as she relayed this story.

After I left on the night we all worked together, Jessica went out to dinner. When she got home, she remembered that she had a good-sized candy cane in a basket in the kitchen. She pulled it out, and Glory's eyes were full and bright. She stared at Jessica as if Jessica had just opened the door to Willy Wonka's Chocolate Factory! Jessica said Glory did a little dance she hadn't done before. When Glory took the candy cane in her mouth, Jessica felt a joyful wave of energy go through her that was so sweet. She was right in the moment with Glory. Jessica was so connected to Glory that she could actually feel every vibration of enthusiasm and sheer joy that Glory experienced. Although Jessica didn't have a candy cane of her own, the moment she shared with Glory was so exquisite to her that I knew the work we did together had been a success. Jessica felt Glory's moment as if it were her own. In turn, Jessica used the energy to fuel her own life. It was truly very sweet indeed.

Glory's story is illustrative of the fact that even when we focus on the lighter side of our connection to our animals, along with the charming traits our animals possess that are unique to them, it is important for us to remember that we can learn as much from these lighter moments as from the neuroses or psychological disturbances. If we work successfully on the connection between our dogs and ourselves, we can feel their joy as strongly as they do. Those moments can be so powerful and beautiful for us. This is because humans tend to lose the ability to have such poignant moments, even about the littlest things. Dogs have that ability. Their energy is alive, flourishing, and balanced. It's beautiful and quite divine.

Toby

In order to keep a clean flow of energy and to stay connected to yourself and your dog, it is so important to be kind to yourself! I will share my visit with Toby as a reminder of that. But first, let's look at what we humans do to ourselves.

We spend so much of our time beating ourselves up, thinking about what we should have done, and berating ourselves. We regress and anxiously focus on all the wrong things we've done in our lives—so much so that we lose perspective and our true light. Please take the time to be gentle with yourself, to be your own best friend, and to support who you are. Listening is an important key. Listen to yourself.

We are unfortunately our own worst enemy and sometimes we don't know how to stop generating the negativity created by our self-criticism. It inhibits all that we do. When we can get ourselves quiet enough to say, "I am hurting myself," or "I am tired and need to have some quiet," then we are connecting to ourselves. Try not to think what you should have done or how you are ill equipped to handle a situation. It throws you out of balance and stops your energy. It creates static energy that hovers, doesn't move, and won't let you move out of it. As your animal is its own energy source, so are you. Keep that in mind. If you degrade or destroy your source energy, then you can't move forward. That's why it's necessary to create moments of time to nurture and take care of that source. This will bring you a much clearer connection to yourself and to all things; a connection that vibrates out and gives you in return what is really necessary for your journey. Trust in knowing this. Your dog makes a point of this daily!

How often do you look down at your dog and see it just quietly cleaning its feet or chewing a bone in absolute joy, completely and utterly involved in its own quiet moment? So much so, that you make a point of it. Dogs take the time to be their own best friend. They enjoy and need it so that when a new moment comes, with an opportunity to take a walk, for example, they have nurtured their soul enough to eagerly move into the next moment. Even dogs that are in tight confined cages, whether in the pound or a rescue facility, take moments to nurture themselves. Although their destiny is not yet evident, they spend time to enjoy and take care of themselves in the process. Dogs don't dwell on or understand "future." They don't worry about what will happen if something else comes up, will they get adopted, or is their food coming. None of that exists while they clean and nurture themselves.

We humans don't know how to do that. We have to book every minute of our time because if we don't, then,

"What if? What if . . . " That's the signal that it's time to let go of control and become neutral. It is essential. We make self-defeating promises that we will take time for ourselves two months from now when we schedule a vacation because we convinced ourselves we can control everything until then. That's how we want it to work, but it doesn't work that way with connective energy. It just doesn't.

Time to nurture and be kind to yourself should not be "scheduled." It is something that needs to be done daily, even in the smallest capacity. Being generally kind to yourself on a daily basis and listening internally means absolutely everything, and dictates what emanates from you. It lends color to the quality of the energy you send out. Again, you are the true source. If you dry up that source or kick it over and over, how do you expect to connect? It is when you find yourself in that moment that you look to and observe your dog. Look carefully as you will learn how to be kind to yourself and live in your truest light. Our friend Toby is the perfect teacher for this parable.

I came to Toby and her human companions Jane and Ronald to address some health issues not only with Toby but for her companions as well. The session was long and quite detailed. We visited the many possible roads that led Toby to Jane and Ronald, and along the way I discovered that Toby was a beautiful, quiet little dog who languished in quality time and sincere nurturing. I also learned that her special alone time that she so loved involved a little stuffed gorilla.

Toby let me know that she really loved a certain stuffed animal. When I relayed this to Jane and Ronald, they nodded "yes." I said it was a stuffed animal that seemed to have arms and legs, and although she had many stuffed animals, she really loved this particular one. When you try to give her something else, she won't accept it. Jane said Toby really loved this little stuffed gorilla and that she had two of them. Whenever Toby was given any other stuffed animals, she would never take to them. All she ever wanted were these two gorillas. She played with them, and then after playing took them away somewhere so she could sit quietly and just stare at them. She put her paw over one, and snuggled with the other. She got lost for quite a long time in nurturing both the gorillas and herself.

I then turned back to Toby. She requested a whole "litter" of gorillas. She wanted six or eight of them. Not because she longed to truly be a mother, but because she had really connected to her own mother who radiated such calm when she nurtured her litter. She didn't feel a loss of her mother, rather, quite the opposite. It was the reliving of a nurturing moment and she felt reconnected. Toby needed and wanted that calm as it was where Toby felt at peace. However, she wouldn't find it with anything else other than those gorillas!

I watched her with the two gorillas. It was extraordinary how she found such a quiet comforting moment. There was no need to judge her choice, or why it worked that way. Toby simply received comfort and peace from the gorillas. As Jane, Ronald, and I looked at her in that moment, she returned the beautiful calming energy to each one of us.

Whatever your "gorilla" is, it is not for anyone (including you) to judge. Just get quiet and enjoy the moment, and that moment will bring many more wonderful moments. You will feel better than you ever imagined. Trust!

Poor Jane and Ronald, who were just so wonderful and open to the process, struggled with the uncertainty of whether they could find more of the exact same gorillas. Toby would not take any imposters. They found the gorilla online, but the last time they checked, there were none left. After our session I did a brief search online to help facilitate the purchase of six gorillas. Lo and behold, I felt I may have found it! I wrote a little email to Jane attaching the link to where I believed the gorilla was for sale. I waited for a response as to whether that was indeed the correct gorilla. Moments later, Jane confirmed I had found it. Jane was elated and such a wonderful participant in this process. She wanted to encourage a calm, emotional state for Toby and set out to purchase six gorillas. Toby now has the "litter" she wanted.

This event only furthered the connection between Jane, Ronald, and Toby. It supported Toby's need to nurture and feel nurtured whenever she had her own alone time, and was necessary for the many other connections that were made that day in our session. Toby was avidly working to produce harmony and good health in the household. She was greatly concerned for Jane and Ronald. She came to them for additional reasons, each of which required Toby to fulfill a job. She was destined to do so.

Jane and Ronald had become connected to Toby's energy, and Toby to theirs. Both Jane and Ronald had a soul retrieval, and identified with the one that occurred for Toby. They saw how crucial it was for Toby to value what is important to her, in both quiet and play time. They support what is important to Toby as Toby supports what is important to them. This keeps everyone clear and connected. The connection allows Toby to appreciate the quality of those moments in a new way so that when she steps out of the moment, she is ever present to continue the journey she is on with Jane and Ronald.

The art of connecting to your dog and then to yourself is a practice. Being aware is a practice. Changing the flow of energy is a practice. I emphasize this because we have all become so obsessed with instant gratification. We have lost sight of everything else. What *is* instant is a real connection to your animal, which opens up a connection to yourself. What is also instant is the energy you put toward your dog, the Universe, and yourself. You suddenly become aware. Being aware and connected changes everything for both you and your dog because your dog's energy has been identified and connected to you. Your dog is right there with you and it's a beautiful feeling for the two of you to know you are in this together.

The work one has to do to stay present and connected is not instant. Yet once we make the connection, our whole life is opened to new avenues we never expected. Taking ownership of various contradictions and inconsistencies within ourselves becomes easier, and we walk down a clearer path because of that awareness. Your energy gets stronger and radiates out to both your dog and to the world. It is clean, connected, and fruitful. When you hit a bump in the road, it is not as discouraging, and you are able to take the right steps to get reconnected. Every time this is done, we are more heightened, and that is what this process is all about. Inevitably this makes you more and more connected to who you really are, why you have chosen your dog, why your dog has chosen you, and what all this has to do with your life in the moment. It is up to you how you will utilize that connection and the energy it generates.

The tools provided here and the practices described to make use of those tools open up limitless possibilities. Your dog is one of the best possible guides you could have to help you navigate your journey of discovery and happiness. Although I am not physically working with you, you have the ability. You are fully equipped. So go ahead. You will be fine. You can do this. Now let's connect.

Chapter Eleven

Steps to Connect

This chapter consists of two sections. The first is a glossary of the most common energetic terms and phrases I use throughout the book. The second is a step-by-step guide for you to refer to when working energetically with your animal.

Glossary

The following terms and phrases are used throughout this book, and their explanation will help you develop a deeper understanding of the energetic process and work I do with my clients and their animals. It is my hope that becoming familiar with these basic terms and following the steps to connect will give you the start you need to help you energetically connect much more easily to your dog and to yourself.

What Is Energy?

An electromagnetic field of energy surrounds all of us and surrounds all existing physical objects. It extends outside the body and cannot be seen using our usual eyesight. It is also called an *aura*. It is a field of light and energy that can be measured and has color. What creates this energy is the rotation or spinning of the energy centers within the body known as *Chakras,* a Sanskrit word meaning *wheel.* It is this energetic field that I work with to connect you to your dog, and reconnect you to yourself.

Chakra Energy Centers

There are seven Chakra energy centers within the body, and their location and meaning differ, depending on which cultural tradition is defining them. This Chakra energy system is a system within the body that is real and exists just like the circulatory or lymph system. It helps define us as human beings because it is the source of our awareness of who we are and how we can change. It is from and to these energy centers that energy is received and transmitted. See the Human Chakra Diagram in Appendix A for the location of each Chakra; and the Chakra Energy and Animal Spirit Chart in Appendix B for a complete explanation of each of the seven traditional energy centers within the body used in energy work, and an explanation of what each of the colored Chakras represent.

How Energy Is Received and Transmitted

We receive energy from or transmit energy to the Chakra energy centers within the body through our hands. The right hand gives or transmits energy, and the left hand receives energy. The left/right nature and function of the hands also correspond with the left/right nature and function of the brain. That is, the left side of the brain deals with language and processes information in a logical and sequential manner. The right side is more visual, and the information is processed intuitively and holistically. In many cultures, the left, or receiving, hand is considered feminine as is the left side of the body, and the right, or giving, hand is considered masculine as is the right side of the body. We do energy work in a state of meditation. So, within a meditative state, when we place our left hand on one of the Chakras within our own bodies, we ask and direct that the energy from that Chakra center be received into the left hand; and similarly, we ask and direct that the energy pass through us and be transmitted out of our right hand into the subject we are working with. In the context of this book, the subject is your dog.

Guides and Animal Spirit Guides

Each human and animal is led through life with spirit guides, either in the form of animal or human, that connect to the subject at the time of birth. I use the terms spirit guide and guides interchangeably. These guides are with either the animal or the human throughout the course of this lifetime and most likely many other lifetimes. We all have them. One must know that although I have the gift to see and hear these guides clearly, someone who is new to energy work may not be able to see or hear them so clearly or possibly not at all. However, it is important to know that anyone has the ability to begin learning how to communicate through energy while in a meditative state as to what guides them and what guides their animals. It is important to know that you do not choose your guides; they choose you. And, as more specifically explained in the "Steps to Connect" section later in this chapter, if your intention is to be open to something larger for yourself and your dog, you have the ability to ask for any guide or spirit guide connected to either you or your dog to make themselves known to you.

Seeing and Hearing an Energetic Presence

What I mean by an energetic presence is a form of energy. It exists within the higher energy frequency that occupies the spirit world. I have the ability to energetically see and hear spirits that are present and make themselves known to me. Sometimes I can see a figure in light, and other times it can be energy alone that allows me to feel whether it is male or female and what species it is. Often it depends on how clear I am. In the metaphysical world, the other factor is what I am meant to see and what I am not. Can you see and hear an energetic presence? The answer is simply yes—if you are open to it and are meant to.

Intention

A great example of the fact that anyone can do energy work is this. We all have the ability to set a solid intention. What we are not always aware of is whether or not we believe in a metaphysical approach. Intention in any form is energy. When one wants to quit smoking after twenty years and tries every method under the sun, and nothing works, one gets frustrated. They want so badly to remove a vice in their life—a behavior that has clearly held them back from a healthy life, and they don't want to exist in that ill health anymore. The day that smoker sets a solid clear intention to stop smoking cold turkey, no matter what the repercussions are, that is a source of energy being sent to remove a block that is clearly slowing you down in your life and inhibiting you from what you want to do—in this case, stop smoking. If the energy and intention are strong and clear enough, that vibration radiates out from your source intention.

Removing an Energy Block

When I use the term "removing the block," what I am referring to is the fact that a block is a stagnant form of energy within the electromagnetic energy field that surrounds each of us. If I were to explain it in a visual context, to me it looks like a ball of darkness, not light. Its presence inhibits the natural flow of energy within the human or the animal. To that extent, when I set out to remove a block, I am focusing my clear energy and intention on what, and specifically where, the block is in both the human and/or the animal. The location and nature of the block can be different for each subject. Once I understand what the blocked energy represents, where it is located, and what is needed to remove it, through a meditative state I set a clear energetic intention to remove the block by using the human's guides as well as the animal's guides that are presented to me in meditation. As I direct my energy to remove the obstructions, I am continually guided by the human's and dog's guides as to the best way to execute that.

Therefore, when I remove an energetic obstruction or block, I never take that on alone. I have the ability to energetically see and hear the spirits that guide either the human or animal. Because the guides know their subjects so intimately, I ask that they energetically communicate to me what the best and most non-invasive method is for me to approach, identify, and remove the blocked energetic source from their subject. Also important to understand is that what needs to be done when I first approach the work to unblock the energetic obstruction is no different than what somebody else (who is new to energy work) has to do.

What most of us don't know is that it is your guides, you, and your energy along with your clear intention that allow the energetic vibration to work to your benefit in the removal of what you deemed as your energetic block. So, when someone asks me, "Can I set that same intention if I can't see what you see, and I can't feel what you feel, but I feel something?" I say to that: "You have the capacity within intention alone to feel what guides you, to understand what guides you, and to remove any block that slows you down in any category of your life." The simplest way to do this is to set a clear intention. That is what I do when I start my work and that is what I hold onto right through the entire healing and/or removal process. This is the easiest way I know to explain to you what I mean by removing a block.

Visualization

Visualization occurs during meditation. On one level, we help create the visualization by focusing, such as visualizing our breath in and out as white light. On a higher level, we are given visions in meditation. What is presented through both vision and sound is what is necessary for us to receive and what is in the moment.

Steps to Connect

The steps presented in this chapter will allow you to work with your dog and yourself, and to accomplish goals gradually. They are provided to guide you to a better understanding of how energy works, and how recognizing and identifying your true connection and soul can propel you and your dog to both a higher level of understanding of who and what you are, and a more beautiful connection to each other. I assure you, the rewards that flow from the effort and the work that you and your dog put forth will be worth every second each of you has given.

The techniques used in meditation are breath, visualization, and intention. The length of time to complete the entire process prior to beginning your removal and/ or healing work varies for each individual depending on one's familiarity with it and how long you have been practicing. My estimate is five to fifteen minutes of preparation. If you are a beginner to these techniques and this process, don't worry about feeling a little confused, lost, or unsure of yourself. Just do the best you can and sense what feels right for you.

Where to Connect

Find a quiet place where you and your dog can sit comfortably. Once physically located, let your intuition guide you to where you need to place your hands on the dog.

Suggestions and Reminders: One thing that may help direct the placement of your hands or guide your intuition is that whenever you are dealing with behavioral issues (for example, anxiety or aggression in any form), it is best to place your right hand on the dog on one of the following three of the seven energy centers (Chakras) within the body through which you will transmit your energy to your dog: (1) the Crown Chakra (top of its head between the ears); or (2) the Heart Chakra (center of chest directly over its heart); or (3) the Solar Plexus Chakra (upper chest, a few inches back from its front legs). That's your best bet. There is no need to place your right hand on the area of the dog's body related to the manifestation of the behavior; you must go to the source. What I mean by this, for example, is in the case of a dog biting too much. You would not place your right hand on its mouth to heal that behavior because that is just the manifestation. The source energy for excessive biting comes from the Heart Chakra, and the placement of your right hand would be over the dog's heart.

To receive energy from or transmit energy to the Chakras within the body through the hands, the right hand gives or transmits energy (through which you transmit the energy to your dog); and the left hand receives energy (through which you receive the energy from the energy centers within your body). See the Human Chakra Diagram in Appendix A for where to place your left hand on your own body.

Breath Control

Close your eyes and go into meditation. You stay in meditation during the entire process. Start taking in long deep breaths while focusing on longer breaths out. Focus on your breath travelling through you and connecting with your dog's breath.

Visualization

After about ten long breaths, start to visualize each breath in and each breath out as white light streaming through both you and your dog. See a merging white light connection between the two of you. Once you can see your breath in this way, put yourself in a completely neutral clear state of mind and energy.

Suggestions and Reminders: If during Visualization you see any colors, or one predominant color, know that these colors are here to guide you. This is something you should pay attention to. The color, or colors, also help lead you to the location on your body and your dog's body where you should place your hands for proper energetic movement. See the Chakra Energy and Animal Spirit Chart in Appendix B for an explanation of what each of the colored Chakras represent (the Chakra colors are the same for both human and dog).

Declarations

Once you are clear and neutral, declare to yourself and to your dog, out loud or silently, that you are open to a connection of energy between you, your dog and the Universe. Know that you and your dog sit in a safe space. Also know that you are ready and open to receive and give clear energy in order to fulfill a higher connection to your dog. At this point, you can begin declaring what you want for yourself and for your dog.

Start Your Focus and Intention

After completing your declarations, you can start focusing on what your main intention is. Define whether it is for removal of a toxic obstruction, erratic behavior, or disconnection affecting you and your dog, or whether it is for nurturing, healing, or simply establishing a pure energetic connection to your dog. As always, it is important to focus on one's breath as white light throughout the whole process of Visualization, Declaration, and Focus and Intention.

Using Guides

This is not as tricky as it sounds. What guides each individual human being and animal can only come to you after you are in a quiet meditative state. How you receive it, when you receive it, or who your guides will be cannot be dictated. You do not choose your guides; they choose you. What I can tell you is this: if your intention is to open to something larger for yourself, for your dog, and for your connection, and that intention never waivers, you have the ability to ask for any animal or spirit guide to have an open path to you and to make themselves known. In what form it is delivered is yet to be seen. All you need to do is be open with clear intention when asking that your guides be made known to you. See the Chakra Energy and Animal Spirit Chart in Appendix B for the identification of the animal guides associated with each Chakra.

What Should I Be Seeing or Hearing?

This is your journey and your dog's journey. That is why it is very important that when you go into Visualization during meditation, you are clear in where you would like to go and what you are open to see. At this point, the Universe is in front of you. If you have achieved a quiet flow of breath and a clear neutral state, what is going to be presented to you through both vision and sound is what is necessary for you to receive and what is in the moment. I know my description of what you will be presented with is not much to hang your hat on, but you are in a metaphysical realm. All you have to do is trust and show up!

How Do I Energetically Remove an Unwanted Issue?

Instructions: Continuing in a quiet meditative state, focus on determining the source of your unwanted issue in life, quietly acknowledge ownership of it, and then declare that it no longer works for you. Then, ask the Universe that it be released immediately from you and your dog. Once that is done, ask for the aid and guidance to become aware and connected to your dog energetically. Speak to your dog and declare to him or her that you shall work to keep yourself free and clear of the unwanted issue, anxiety, or neurosis that could cause harm or create an unnatural state for you or your dog. Take deep breaths throughout this whole process and visualize the breaths as white light. Once done, always, always, always say thank you.

Suggestions and Reminders: Deep-seated anxiety in one's dog definitely has a direct correlation to a deep hidden energy within you. When focusing on removing an unwanted issue (aggression, neurosis, or anxiety, for example) in yourself, your dog, your home, or all three, it is very important that you give yourself the ability to see and take ownership of the source of the issue. From that moment forward, you will become aware of any energy from within or outside yourself that further fuels that issue. This awareness is what enables you to recognize the source, understand it, and remove it.

For placement of your hands during the removal process, please see the Suggestions and Reminder section under the "Where to Connect" heading earlier in this chapter for any behavioral problems you wish to remove. If the issue is a medical condition, then use your judgment and your intuition to guide you in where to place your hands. For example, if your dog is recovering from a broken leg and is uncomfortable, then let your intuition guide you with the help of your dog's energy and what the dog wants from you as to whether your hand should be directly or lightly placed on or nearby the leg that is injured. Wherever it is comfortable for you and your dog to work is where you place your hands.

How to Nurture and Heal

The steps for nurturing and healing are the same as those listed under the heading "How Do I Energetically Remove an Unwanted Issue?" The only difference between the two is your intention. In removal, you intended to remove an unwanted issue or obstruction; here your intention is to pass nurturing healing energy to help heal an illness (whether physical, mental, emotional, or spiritual), behavioral problem, or stress-related issue.

Instructions: To receive energy from yourself to transmit to your dog, place your left hand on your Solar Plexus Chakra (again, it is in the abdominal region between your rib cage and your navel), quietly go into deeper breath, make your intention, find the place in you that needs healing under that same intention, and hold that. Continually breathe through white light into your left hand through your Solar Plexus Chakra with that very intention for yourself and yourself only. Once you start feeling a new fresh energy circulating throughout your Solar Plexus Chakra, take ownership of what you would like to heal within yourself. Then ask the Universe to be connected to your dog using both your energies to heal one another in the same intention. I guarantee that whatever you believe needs to be healed within yourself will need to be healed within your dog as well.

While staying in meditation, let your intention guide your right hand to be placed on your dog wherever you energetically feel you have the most strength and connection on the dog to adequately send the energy emanating from your Solar Plexus Chakra to the dog. Hear and see where it is comfortable for your dog to receive the energy from you. Only you will know that. Throughout this whole process, your left hand remains constantly on your Solar Plexus Chakra until the process is completed.

When you are ready to move out of the healing work you have just done, you must declare out loud or silently that both you and your dog ask to be released of any energetic blocks that could bring either of you back to an unhealthy static state. Once the Nurturing and Healing work is done, the intention never changes; even out of a meditative state.

Suggestions and Reminders: Because Nurturing and Healing is a more focused energetic process, it is very important to note the clarity of your breath, the white light of your breath that you see through Visualization, and the intention of the directed energy. The only way to heal or remove an energetic obstruction or issue on a very deep level, whether within your animal or utilizing your animal's energy to remove it within yourself, it is very important to continually and simultaneously focus on the following: (1) be very clear that the energy circulating is consistently within white light; (2) hold your intention and be in complete awareness throughout the process; and (3) the human being must take ownership of and identify the energetic obstruction or issue within themselves through meditation. If you cannot find the source of the issue within yourself, it will be very hard for you to have power within your energy Chakras to connect to, remove an energetic obstruction, or heal your dog.

If you find that it is hard for you to see your energy in a clear white light, or feel the flow of energy between you and your dog, or stay in meditation while carrying out the process, it is important to take a moment, remove your hands from both yourself and your dog, and get yourself centered before you go back into meditation and begin again. Although intention is important throughout, when it comes to nurturing and healing, I cannot stress enough the importance of one's clarity, breath, higher connection, and ability to stay present within meditation.

This specific nurturing and healing process requires practice. It will never be instant. Once you have understood how to locate, identify, use, and transmit your energy correctly, I guarantee you will feel within you the energetic shift resulting from that understanding the moment you have done so.

Once you start moving energy between you and your dog to heal you both, and once the neurosis is removed from you and your dog in that healing process, going forward you can ask for your dog to become your guide, your mentor, and your teacher for the purpose of helping you and your dog stay in the proper clear light the two of you have created. Then you will be able to make declarations through your energetic connection for both of you to continually have and maintain a healthy energetic healing response.

Moving Out of the Process

Once the removal and healing processes are complete, it is important, before removing your hands from yourself and your dog, and stepping out of the meditative state, to declare protection of white light for, and all around, both you and your dog. Never release from fresh energy without protecting everything that was involved in the process. Tell your dog that once you take your hand off its body and complete the process, you will stay connected to each other by mind, body, spirit, and eternal energy as you both move forward. With your eyes still closed, slowly step out of the meditative state, relax your hands, and pet your dog. Quietly thank him for being in your life. Tell him that you accept his guidance and support as well as his love, and that you return it equally. Declare an openness to the energetic connection between the two of you from that moment on.

Giving Thanks

It is as simple as that. Whenever you are done with a Metaphysical journey or experience like this, it is always important to say thank you to yourself, your dog, and anything higher that you believe in that guided and aided you in the process. Just say "Thank you."

Appendix A
Human Chakra Diagram

7. *The Crown Chakra*
(Crown or Top of Head)

6. *The Third Eye Chakra*
(Middle Forehead Between Brows)

5. *The Throat Chakra*
(Throat and Neck)

4. *The Heart Chakra*
(Directly over Heart, Center of Chest)

3. *The Solar Plexus Chakra*
(Abdomen, Between Navel and Ribs)

2. *The Sacral Chakra*
(Base of Spine)

1. *The Base/Root Chakra*
(Genitals)

Appendix B
Chakra Energy and Animal Spirit Chart

CHAKRA	LOCATION	REPRESENTS	COLOR	ANIMAL SPIRIT	ANIMAL ASSOCIATION
SEVENTH (Crown)	Crown or Top of Head	Oneness, Spirituality, Ascension, Consciousness	**VIOLET PURPLE**		Power, Exploration, Illumination, Clarity of Vision
SIXTH (Third Eye)	Middle Forehead (Above and Between the Brows)	Universal Truth, Intuition, Life Energy, Dreams	**INDIGO**		Rebirth, Transition, Ability to Observe the Unseen
FIFTH (Throat)	Throat and Neck	Self-Power, Expression, Harmony, Eloquence	**BLUE**		Royalty, Intelligence, Removal of Obstacles and Barriers
FOURTH (Heart Center)	Heart (Center of Chest)	Unconditional Love, Compassion, Forgiveness, Acceptance	**GREEN**		Strength, Confidence, Shape Shifting, Facing Fears
THIRD (Solar Plexus)	Abdominal Region (Between Navel and Rib Cage)	Personal Power, Control, Survival	**YELLOW**		Growth, Fearlessness, Medicine Magic, Self-Knowledge
SECOND (Sacral)	Base of Spine	Physical Desires, Emotional Balance, Addictions, Appetite	**ORANGE**		Vulnerability, Aggressiveness, Link to Plant and Animal Spirits
FIRST (Root or Base)	Gonads (Genitals)	Survival, Material and Monetary Concerns, Tribal/Familial Issues, Physical Needs	**RED**		Guardian of Lower Regions, Connector with Earth's Energies, Sensitive to Touch and Vibration

About the Author

Jocelyn Kessler lives in Los Angeles with her dog Emma and works both in California and New York with animals and their owners, including many high-profile individuals. A great lover of all animals and the outdoors, Jocelyn can be found in her spare time taking long walks with her dog Emma, writing, cooking, meditating and thoroughly enjoying this wonderful journey.

Visit Jocelyn at *www.jocelynkessler.com.*

Hampton Roads Publishing Company

. . . for the evolving human spirit

Hampton Roads Publishing Company publishes books
on a variety of subjects, including spirituality, health,
and other related topics.

For a copy of our latest trade catalog, call
(978) 465-0504 or visit our distributor's website at
www.redwheelweiser.com. You can also sign up for our
newsletter and special offers by going to
www.redwheelweiser.com/newsletter/.